FINDING VICTO

JESUS

THE ANCHOR
OF OUR SOULS

BIBLE STUDY AND WORKBOOK

DEBORAH BEDSON

JESUS THE ANCHOR OF OUR SOULS BIBLE STUDY AND WORKBOOK

Cover Design by 100Covers.com

DEDICATION

My heartfelt thanks for those who have encouraged me to write, write, write! I pray you will enjoy the fruits of my labor.

And especially to my Lord and Savior, Jesus Christ. Thank you for patiently and gently guiding me to put YOUR words on paper and loving me through my stubbornness to do it my way. Will I never learn?

GOING DEEPER

This book is meant to be used as a supplement to a regular Bible reading plan.

To dig deeper into God's Word and to make your study richer, it is recommended that you read each passage listed in its full context. That is, read the entire chapter the scripture is pulled from.

FREE RESOURCE

If you would like to have corresponding journal pages, with space provided for each bible passage, you can email me at:

deborah@deborahbedsonauthor.com

Or check out my website: **www.deborahbedsonauthor.com** and sign up there. A pdf file will be sent to you that you can download and print.

LET'S CONNECT

Please check out my social media sites:

www.deborahbedsonauthor.com Here you will get updates on my new projects, find recommended resources and a sign up for my weekly emails.

www.letstalkaboutjesusblog.blogspot.com catch up on my weekly blog posts about life with Jesus, weekly bible memory verses and other cool stuff!

Join my Facebook group, **It's All About Jesus The Living Word.** Here we share updates, prayer requests and praise reports, and have a fun time interacting with other believers, encouraging and strengthening the brethren! But mostly it is a place where Jesus is honored.

TABLE OF CONTENTS

"This hope we have as an anchor of the soul, both sure and steadfast, and which enters the Presence behind the veil, where the forerunner has entered for us, even Jesus, having become High Priest forever according to the order of Melchizedek."

(Hebrews 6:19-20)

INTRODUCTION

Unless you have been living off the grid somewhere in outer Mongolia, no doubt you have been impacted one way or another by the insanity that seems to have taken over the planet.

For the past three years, we have experienced a never-ending worldwide pandemic called "Covid 19" and all its mutations, racial tensions in this country that rival the 'sixties, and a political landscape that is like a minefield. Let's not even go into the debates on abortion, gun rights, or sexual lifestyles. The very foundation that this nation was built on is being shaken down to the studs. Life as we have known it for the past 200+ years is dangerously close to being taken away from us.

To be honest, there are times when I get so overwhelmed with what I hear I want to stick my head in the sand and pretend it isn't there. There is one problem with that. No, actually two. The first one is that when you eventually come up for air, you will find that the problems surrounding you are still there, maybe even worse. We cannot pretend adversity does not exist or wish it away. Secondly, you get sand in your ears! Most unpleasant….

So how do we keep from going down the slippery slope of despair, anger, or apathy? How do we stay calm and hopeful in a seemingly hopeless world? Do we turn off the news and go about our business? Do we numb the pain with artificial substances, hoping for just a few moments of sweet relief? Or maybe curling up in a ball and refusing to get out of bed works. I don't think so.....

The world will offer many solutions. Join a protest, sign a petition, wear a mask, rant on social media. But at the end of the day, it is fruitless. None of that truly addresses or changes the problems we are facing. The bottom line is there will always be something upsetting our serenity. In John 16:33, Jesus said this: ".... In the world, you will have tribulation..." Wonderful. Isn't that good news! Ah, but if we keep reading, Jesus adds this "But be of good cheer, I have overcome the world." That is indeed good news!

What it all boils down to is that we cannot solve the problems of our world, whether it be global or just our little piece of it, with earthly measures. We can try putting a band-aid on them. But, like the story of the kid putting his finger in the dike to plug up one hole, there is always another one ready to spring open. You only have so many fingers and toes. Sooner or later, you will be overwhelmed and feeling helpless.

So what is the solution to coping with the insanity of life? It is very simple. Jesus Christ and His Word. Nothing more, nothing less, nothing else. Let me give you some examples:

- Are you afraid? *"Be anxious for nothing..."* (Philippians 4:6)
- Money woes? *"And my God shall supply all your need..."* (Philippians 4:19)
- Feeling weak? *"My grace is sufficient for you, for My strength is made perfect in weakness."* (2 Corinthians 12:9)
- Feeling alone? *"...For He Himself has said, "I will never leave you nor forsake you."* (Hebrews 13:5)

These passages are just the tip of the iceberg of what we can find in God's Word. But please do not misunderstand me. I am not suggesting that if we read a bible verse and believe it, then all of a sudden the problem goes away. I am not in the camp of the "Name it and claim it" group. God is not a magic genie just waiting to serve us. But we will find the peace, strength, hope, and comfort in His Word that we will not find anywhere else. There is something else that I can guarantee. If you embrace God's Word and live out His teachings, there will be a change in your heart that will transform how you do this thing called life. And your life will become fruitful and fulfilling. This, in itself, will go a long way to changing your little piece of real estate on planet Earth. I would be willing to bet it may change others around you as well! Here is another, even better promise. You will be storing up treasures in heaven!

The Purpose of this Book:
My goal in writing this book is to help equip you, the reader, with an arsenal of weapons to combat and be victorious against the trials you are facing. Any issue we have is addressed in the Bible. We just have to seek it out. And that is exactly what we will do. We will dig deep into the scriptures for truth.

I don't believe Jesus called me to write this book to tell you how to solve your problems. Or to interpret the scriptures for you. My job here is to lead you to the One who CAN. Jesus and His Word. The format is this: Each chapter will address an issue that most of us struggle with at some time or another. The Bible will be our textbook. The chapter will begin with an "anchor" scripture that we will springboard from. There will be several bible passages that relate to the chapter's topic. You will be asked to study each passage and journal your discoveries. There is space for writing out your answers. There will then be some reflection questions to answer then the chapter will wrap up with a "call to action".

Every chapter has 14 unique scripture passages related to the topic. Why the number 14? "Experts" say the number 14 represents completion, spiritual perfection, and biblical significance. But not everything has a spiritual slant. I think my OCD kicked in!

Here's a helpful suggestion: the more you put into the study, the more you will get out of it. Of course, it is entirely up to you, but the only way you will grow in God's Word is to dig into it.

So it needs to be more than just academic. You have to put the work in if you want to grow. Like gardening, you cannot just throw seeds in the ground and expect to have a bountiful harvest. There is some effort required. But the rewards will be worth it, I promise!

**I highly recommend that you get a journal or a notebook. It's a great way to record additional thoughts that you have, and you will need it for your "Call to Action" at the end of each devotional.

** To get the most benefit from the passages, read the entire chapter the scripture is pulled from. This will help you with the context of the Word. Write down thoughts and revelations in your journal. Extra points if you do what is called an inductive study. Here is one method called S.O.A.P:

STEP 1: SCRIPTURE: Read the assigned passage. I highly recommend reading at least a few verses before and after to understand the context.
STEP 2: OBSERVATION: What do you observe while reading it?
STEP 3: APPLICATION: How can you apply this to your life today?
STEP 4: PRAYER: Write a prayer based on your observation and application.

I have provided a free resource to help you journal your thoughts using this study method. Just go to **www.deborahbedsonauthor.com** Request the free resource and you will be emailed a PDF File. There is a page for each passage we study. Print it out and you are ready to go! So grab your Bible and let's get started with the foundation of prayer. Happy studying!

CHAPTER 1

PRAYER-OUR GREATEST WEAPON

"If My people who are called by My name will humble themselves, and pray and seek My face, and turn from their wicked ways, then I will hear from heaven, and will forgive their sin and heal their land." (2 Chronicles 7:14)

ANY SUCCESSFUL JOURNEY BEGINS WITH preparation. Oh, I remember a family vacation one time where, let's just say, the menfolk neglected their duties of making sure the family motorhome was in good condition for our trip. Not thirty miles away from home, we had our first problem. A flat tire. Then the next day, a belt broke. It seemed every day something went wrong. A little maintenance before we left would have gone a long way toward safer travels!

As we start this journey to a closer relationship with Jesus, we have some pre-trip maintenance to do ourselves. Our main vehicle is going to be prayer. This is like the gas in the engine. But we can't just lift up a prayer and let it go at that, expecting God to respond. He has a checklist of His own.

Read the opening scripture again. Note the criteria He is asking for:
1.   Humble ourselves. We have to approach the throne of heaven with a broken spirit. We cannot be haughty or proud.

2. We need to pray and seek His face. "Arrow" prayers that are just shot up there halfheartedly are not what He is looking for from us. We need to engage our hearts in this two-way relationship.
3. Turn from our wicked ways. Sin is like slime in a backed-up drain. It clogs the pipe and prevents the clean water from flowing freely.

HEART PREPARATION

So our first call to action is to cry out to the Lord. Here are some preparation scriptures for us to consider:

"Search me, O God, and know my heart; try me, and know my anxieties; and see if there is any wicked way in me, and lead me in the way everlasting." (Psalm 139:23-24).

"Who may ascend into the hill of the Lord? Or who may stand in His holy place? He who has clean hands and a pure heart, who has not lifted up his soul to an idol, nor sworn deceitfully." (Psalm 24:3-4)

"The righteous cry out, and the Lord hears, and delivers them out of all their troubles. The Lord is near to those who have a broken heart, and saves such as have a contrite spirit." (Psalm 34:17-18)

These passages speak of a heart that comes to the throne of God in humility, brokenness, and purity. We cannot harbor unrepentant sin, anger, or have a self-righteous attitude. We have to lay it all aside, seek His forgiveness for our sins, and humbly sit before Him.

FERVENT PRAYERS

We must be engaged with the Lord in our prayer time. Do you have a passion for prayer? Do you long to hear from the Father, and for Him to hear you? Or do you simply toss up the prayer and hope it sticks?

To see the Lord working in our lives, we need a healthy, strong relationship with Him. We need to engage ourselves. What would it be like if you never spent much time talking to your kids, or only gave them a passing glance? Wouldn't you wonder later why they aren't giving back to you in the relationship? A healthy and strong marriage requires honest and genuine communication. Well, so does our relationship with our heavenly Father.

He doesn't want us to give Him a token wave as we carry on with our day. He wants to engage with us.

"...The effective, fervent prayer of a righteous man avails much." (James 5:16b) We need to pray from the depths of our hearts.

"...Father, thank you for hearing me." (John 11:41b) This is the prayer that Jesus prayed before calling Lazarus out of the tomb. It was a prayer of thanksgiving for His Father always hearing Him. Notice it wasn't a long dissertation on prayers of thanksgiving. It was just from the heart. Those are the best ones, in my opinion!

PRAY WITH EXPECTANCY

When you pray, it's important that you believe that your Father will hear you and answer. Pray with the certainty (remembering that clean heart) that He hears your cry. We are also instructed to keep praying, not just a one-time request. But we also need to remember that we are to pray for the Father's will to be done. He only wants the best for us. He won't give us everything we need simply because we ask for it. He won't indulge us. He is the Holy of Holies, the Almighty God. He knows all things, and He has a plan.

"Pray without ceasing." (1 Thessalonians 5:17) Being in an attitude of prayer communication with the Lord is vital to a healthy prayer life.

"So I say to you, ask, and it will be given to you; seek, and you will find; knock, and it will be opened to you. For everyone who asks receives, and he who seeks finds, and to him who knocks it will be opened." (Luke 11:9-10) When you come to God for prayer, ask, seek, and knock until your knuckles are worn down and your knees are bloodied! Or until He answers, anyway. Don't give up too soon. You could be just one prayer away from victory!

"Now this is the confidence that we have in Him, that if we ask anything according to His will, He hears us." (1 John 5:14) Don't miss the key words "according to His will". This isn't an open invitation to get us anything we want. Otherwise, you might experience the next verse:

"You ask and do not receive, because you ask amiss, that you may spend it on your pleasures." (James 4:3) We always want to be praying in God's will, because He knows what is better for us than we do!

"But you, when you pray, go into your room, and when you have shut your door, pray to your Father who is in the secret place; and your Father who sees in secret will reward you openly. And when you pray, do not use vain repetitions as the heathen do. For they think that they will be heard for their many words." (Matthew 6:6-8) Private heartfelt prayers can be so powerful. Carve out some quiet time with the Lord and just pour out your heart to Him.

"So He Himself often withdrew into the wilderness and prayed." (Luke 5:16) Jesus knew the importance of that intimate time of prayer with His Father. We should follow His example.

CONCLUSION

So the first step in finding victory in any situation is to come to the Lord in prayer. Seek Him first, and put aside any prideful thoughts. Be humble and willing to hear from Him. Just remember what He said in Isaiah 55:8-9:

"'For My thoughts are not your thoughts, nor are your ways My ways' says the Lord. 'For as the heavens are higher than the earth, So are My ways higher than your ways, and My thoughts than your thoughts.'"

Thank You Jesus for that! Amen?

"I have called upon You, for You will hear me, O God; Incline Your ear to me, and hear my speech." (Psalm 17:6)

BIBLE STUDY AND JOURNAL TIME

Grab your bible, and dig into the chapter's scriptures! Don't forget to read the entire chapter to get the context. And record what the Lord has revealed to you in each passage. Pray for revelation before you begin.

2 CHRONICLES 7:14 ("Anchor" passage)

_____
_____
_____
_____
_____
_____
_____
_____

PSALM 139:23-24

_____
_____
_____
_____
_____
_____

PSALM 24:3-4

_____
_____
_____
_____
_____
_____
_____

Psalm 34:17-18

_____
_____
_____
_____
_____
_____
_____
_____
_____

JAMES 5:16

_____
_____
_____
_____
_____
_____
_____
_____

JOHN 11:41

_____
_____
_____
_____
_____
_____
_____
_____
_____

1 THESSALONIANS 5:17

_____
_____
_____
_____
_____
_____
_____
_____

LUKE 11:9-10

_____
_____
_____
_____
_____
_____
_____
_____

1 JOHN 5:14

_____
_____
_____
_____
_____
_____
_____
_____

JAMES 4:3

_____

_____

_____

_____

_____

_____

_____

_____

MATTHEW 6:6-8

_____

_____

_____

_____

_____

_____

_____

_____

LUKE 5:16

_____

_____

_____

_____

_____

_____

_____

_____

ISAIAH 55:8-9

_____

_____

_____

_____

_____

_____

_____

_____

_____

PSALM 17:6

_____

_____

_____

_____

_____

_____

_____

_____

_____

Now, summarize what you have learned through the passages. Look for a common theme. Use your journal if you need more space.

_____

_____

_____

_____

_____

_____

_____

_____

_____

_____

_____

_____

_____

_____

_____

_____

_____

_____

_____

_____

_____

_____

_____

_____

_____

_____

_____

_____

_____

_____

REFLECTION TIME

Take your prayer life temperature. How would you honestly rate your communication with the Lord?

_____

_____

_____

_____

_____

What steps can you take to improve the weaker areas of your prayer life?

_____

_____

_____

_____

_____

What passage resonated with you the most and why?

_____

_____

_____

_____

_____

Write out a prayer asking God to reveal to you where there is anything hindering your prayer life, and ask Him to help you to commit to a regular time of prayer with Him.

_____

_____

_____

_____

_____

Heavenly Father:

We thank You that we have the ability to come boldly to the throne and pour out our hearts and our praises to You directly. There is no longer a veil hiding Your face from us. That was made possible by the sacrifice of Your Son on the cross. Help us to take this privilege seriously. Sometimes we can be cavalier about seeking You. Please forgive us of our sins, and reveal the areas of our hearts that need to be cleaned out so that we can come to You in purity. We thank You and we praise You. Amen!

CALL TO ACTION!

Your first assignment of this study is to create a prayer plan.

- Set aside a special time of the day that you will sit down and focus on praying to the Lord. Commit to this!
- Before you start praying, seek forgiveness for any sins you may be harboring. You want to start with a clean slate.
- Praise Him for His goodness. Make a list of things to pray about.
- Write these prayer requests in your journal. But don't treat it like a laundry list of requests. Share them with the Lord. Talk them over. Just like you might be sitting down with a friend.
- Have your Bible handy. Record any scriptures the Holy Spirit may reveal to you.
- Be prepared to listen. Remember, this is a conversation, not a monologue!
- Something I like to do before I start and to end the session, is to lift up a praise song to Him. It goes a long way to prepare your heart, and to seal it.

READY, SET, GO!

CHAPTER 2

WHERE ARE YOU, JESUS?

"When you pass through the waters, I will be with you; and through the rivers, they shall not overflow you. When you walk through the fire, you shall not be burned, nor shall the flame scorch you. For I am the Lord your God." (Isaiah 43:2-3a)

HAVE YOU EVER FELT THAT no matter how hard you try, you just don't feel the presence of the Lord? That is a scary place to be if you are in a desperate situation.

In my previous book, I shared a story of being overwhelmed with fear (self-imposed for sure!) while I was driving on a mountain road in the dark. I was crying out to the Lord, but I didn't feel Jesus with me. I knew in my head that He was there, guiding and protecting me. But I was wrapped up in my circumstances, not allowing Him to comfort me.

Sometimes we get so overwhelmed by our situation that we cannot see what is around us. It feels like we are caught in a riptide that is pulling us under the current. But what do lifeguards tell you to do when that happens or when they are trying to pull you out of the waves? They tell you to relax; to let go of the struggle and let them do their job. But that can be a frightening thing to do. We fear that we are going to go under and never come out again. It's hard to put your trust in others when you think you are drowning!

Do you remember the story of Peter and the other disciples when they were fishing and saw Jesus walking on the water? At first, they were very frightened because they thought they saw a ghost. But Jesus said, "Don't worry guys-it's me!" So Peter (my favorite Bible character-he's so human!), says to Jesus, *"And Peter answered Him and said, 'Lord, if it is You, command me to come to You on the water.'"* (Matthew 14:28)

So Jesus told him to come. Everything started out fine until Peter took his eyes off of Jesus and onto the waves crashing around him. *"But when he saw that the wind was boisterous, he was afraid; and beginning to sink he cried out, saying, 'Lord, save me!'"* (verse 29). Jesus did just that. He grabbed Peter's hand and plucked him out of the water.

So what happened here? What caused Peter to sink? It certainly wasn't Jesus abandoning him. He was right there, standing on the water. No, it was Peter who changed. He started out fully trusting Jesus. But when he took his eyes off his Lord and focused on the waves crashing around him, he panicked and started to sink like a rock. Happy ending, though. He heard Jesus speak, saw His outstretched hand, and trust came back into his heart.

The important thing to remember about this story is that Jesus never left Peter to drown. He was there the entire time, holding His hand out to Peter. It was Peter who moved away from Jesus. That is, his faith and trust in Him disappeared in the circumstance.

We do that a lot, don't we? We can talk all day about how we trust in Jesus when everything is going well and there is nothing but blue skies on the horizon. But when that unforeseen storm hits, our faith is being tested. We start to panic, we cannot see a way out, and suddenly we are like the guy being pulled down in the riptide. The more we fight it, the harder it gets. We need to breathe, seek the Lord, and trust Him that He will see us through the storm.

Here is a passage that offers great comfort to me:
"Hear my cry, O God; attend to my prayer. From the end of the earth I will cry to You. When my heart is overwhelmed, lead me to the rock that is higher than I. For You have been a shelter for me, A strong tower from the enemy. I will abide in Your tabernacle forever; I will trust in the shelter of Your wings." (Psalm 61:1-4) Isn't that a beautiful

18

prayer? Jesus is our Rock, our Shelter, our Strong Tower. I picture Him holding me in His arms and covering me with His love and His protection.

The one thing that you can always count on is the promise of Jesus that He will never forsake us. He knows what we are going through. He is aware of our fears and struggles. We have a choice. We can listen to the taunts of the enemy when he says there is no hope, and that Jesus doesn't care that we are going under. Or we can trust in God's Word:

"Fear not, for I am with you; be not dismayed, for I am your God. I will strengthen you, yes, I will help you, I will uphold you with My righteous right hand." (Isaiah 41:10) We also want to remember that even in the storms that we will inevitably find ourselves in, He is the peace IN the storm.

"In my distress I called upon the LORD, and cried out to my God; He heard my voice from His temple, and my cry came before Him, even to His ears. (Psalm 18:6) God will always hear our cry from the heights of heaven. Crying out to Him should always be our first response.

"And the Lord, He is the One who goes before you. He will be with you, He will not leave you nor forsake you; do not fear nor be dismayed." (Deuteronomy 31:8) This was what Moses told Joshua when he handed over the reins to lead the Israelites into the Promised Land. I am sure there were many times when Joshua clung to this promise!

"For He Himself has said, 'I will never leave you nor forsake you.' So we may boldly say 'The Lord is my helper; I will not fear. What can man do to me?'" (Hebrews 13:5b-6). Okay, I can hear you now, saying, "I will tell you exactly what man can do to me!" Then the enemy puts a whole laundry list in your mind of what can happen to you. Let me give you this to consider: God is bigger than ANYTHING the enemy or the world can throw at you. And there is nothing the enemy can do that God can't prevent.

"...so that they should seek the Lord, in the hope that they might grope for Him and find Him, though He is not far from each one of

us; for in Him we live and move and have our being, as also some of your own poets have said, 'For we are also His offspring'". (Acts 17:27-28) We don't have to look very far to find Him. Like a loving parent, He is always right there with us.

"The Lord is near to all who call upon Him, to all who call upon Him in truth." (Psalm 145:18) We must sincerely seek Him.

"And those who know Your name will put their trust in You; for You, Lord, have not forsaken those who seek You." (Psalm 9:10) Trust Him and seek Him. He'll show up for you!

"All that the Father gives Me will come to Me, and the one who comes to Me I will by no means cast out." (John 6:37) If you are a child of His, He will never cast you aside.

 "And lo, I am with you always, even to the end of the age." (Matthew 28:20b) This was the promise Jesus gave to His disciples before He ascended to heaven. We can hold onto this promise as well.

One more promise to hold onto:
"The secret of the Lord is with those who fear Him, and He will show them His covenant. My eyes are ever toward the Lord, for He shall pluck my feet out of the net." (Psalm 25:14-15)

Please remember that no matter how frightening or discouraging your situation may be, Jesus is always there right beside you. Just reach out your hand, and call to Him. He will lift you up and sustain you.

"But from there you will seek the LORD your God, and you will find Him if you seek Him with all your heart and with all your soul." (Deuteronomy 4:29)

BIBLE STUDY AND JOURNAL TIME

Grab your bible, and dig into the chapter's scriptures! Don't forget to read the entire chapter to get the context. And record what the Lord has revealed to you in each passage. Pray for revelation before you begin.

ISAIAH 43:2-3a ("Anchor" passage)

_____
_____
_____
_____
_____
_____
_____
_____

MATTHEW 14:28-29

_____
_____
_____
_____
_____
_____
_____
_____

PSALM 61:1-4

_____
_____
_____
_____
_____
_____
_____

ISAIAH 41:10

_____
_____
_____
_____
_____
_____
_____
_____
_____

PSALM 18:6

_____
_____
_____
_____
_____
_____
_____
_____

DEUTERONOMY 31:8

_____
_____
_____
_____
_____
_____
_____
_____

HEBREWS 13:5b-6

_____
_____
_____
_____
_____
_____
_____
_____
_____

ACTS 17:27-28

_____
_____
_____
_____
_____
_____
_____
_____

PSALM 145:18

_____
_____
_____
_____
_____
_____
_____
_____

PSALM 9:10

_____
_____
_____
_____
_____
_____
_____
_____
_____

JOHN 6:37

_____
_____
_____
_____
_____
_____
_____
_____

MATTHEW 28:20b

_____
_____
_____
_____
_____
_____
_____
_____

Psalm 25:14-15

_____

_____

_____

_____

_____

_____

_____

_____

DEUTERONOMY 4:29

_____

_____

_____

_____

_____

_____

_____

_____

Now, summarize below what you have learned through the passages. Look for a common theme.

_____

_____

_____

_____

_____

_____

_____

_____

_____

_____

_____

_____

_____

_____

_____

_____

_____

_____

_____

_____

_____

_____

_____

_____

_____

_____

_____

_____

_____

_____

_____

_____

REFLECTION TIME

Have you had a "Peter moment" when you started out trusting Jesus, but that trust failed you during the difficulty? How did you find your way back into that trusting relationship with Jesus?

_____

_____

_____

_____

_____

_____

How does knowing that God is the shelter in your storm help you to cope with your trial?

_____

_____

_____

_____

_____

Review the opening scripture (Isaiah 42:2-3). Think about each scenario. How does this promise of God give you comfort and peace?

_____

_____

_____

_____

_____

Write a prayer thanking God for His promises, and ask Him to be with you in the next storm.

_____

_____

_____

_____

_____

_____

Thank You, Jesus, that no matter what we are going through, You are faithful in Your promise that You will never leave us nor forsake us. Sometimes we cannot feel Your presence. But it is not because You have abandoned us. Help us to trust that You are there, walking beside us, working in the situation for Your perfect purpose. Give us strength for the trials, keep us safe under Your wing, and let us know that we will be victorious because we are Your children.

In Your precious name we pray, Amen!

CALL TO ACTION!

Okay, grab your journal and put on your thinking cap. I want you to think of a difficult trial that you have been through. Describe how you felt while going through it. Be honest about your feelings. If you felt abandoned by God, write that down. He already knows you felt that. What was going on in your head and heart? Did you earnestly seek Him through prayer and scripture? Or did you struggle to figure it out on your own?

Then think about how you got through it. In light of our scriptures today, think about how He was indeed there for you. Thank Him for that.

Finally, come up with a game plan for the trial that is right around the corner. How will you respond when it gets difficult? What scriptures are you going to put in your arsenal to call on? Remember that prayer time you set aside in Chapter 1. Start seeking Him in advance to be with you, to equip you and praise Him for what He is going to do in you and through you. Don't let the purpose of the trial be lost. Gain something from it. Amen?

READY, SET, GO!

CHAPTER 3

FACING YOUR GIANTS

"Then David said to the Philistine, 'You come to me with a sword, with a spear, and with a javelin. But I come to you in the name of the LORD of hosts, the God of the armies of Israel, whom you have defied.'" (1 Samuel 17:45)

TODAY'S SCRIPTURE IS PART OF a well-known Bible story. I am sure you are familiar with it. This gargantuan brute named Goliath came with the Philistine army to take on the army of Saul. Everyone was afraid of him because of his size. Well, almost everyone. Enter shepherd boy David! But he was not doing this in his own strength or through pride. He knew that God was on his side. He had his marching orders. And he didn't fight with powerful weapons, but with a simple little slingshot. The rest is history.

We face our own giants every day. They take on many forms. Doubt, fear, failure, health issues, marriage woes, prodigal kids, money, or lack of it. They feel insurmountable. And sometimes they seem to snowball and you feel like you are getting piled upon! So how do we look at these problems? Here is an interesting contrast taken from the Book of Numbers. Spies were sent to scout the land. Here was their report:

"And they gave the children of Israel a bad report of the land which they had spied out, saying, 'The land through which we have gone as spies is a land that devours its inhabitants, and all the people whom we saw in it are men of great stature. There we saw the giants (the descendants of Anak came from the giants), and we were like

grasshoppers in our own sight, and so we were in their sight.'" (Numbers 13:32-33) They basically said, "We are overmatched!"

But Joshua and Caleb had also gone with them and gave this report:
"...The land we passed through to spy out is an exceedingly good land. If the Lord delights in us, then He will bring us into this land and give it to us, a land which flows with milk and honey. Only do not rebel against the Lord, nor fear the people of the land, for they are our bread; their protection has departed from them, and the Lord is with us. Do not fear them." (Numbers 14:7-9)

What can we glean from this? There is an important lesson here. Please note that everyone saw the same thing. So why was the main group so frightened, but Joshua and Caleb were so confident? I give you this for consideration: The spies were looking at the problem from a human perspective. When we try to do things in our own strength, the problems may really look like giants. Then yes, we are like grasshoppers, and our troubles seem insurmountable. But note what Joshua said. "The Lord is with us." If God is with us, then how can we be anything but victorious?

"Then all this assembly shall know that the Lord does not save with sword and spear; for the battle is the Lord's, and He will give you into our hands." (1 Samuel 17:47)

"For the Lord your God is He who goes with you, to fight for you against your enemies, to save you." (Deuteronomy 20:4)

"You must not fear them, for the Lord your God Himself fights for you." (Deuteronomy 3:22)

I find these words very comforting. It gives a sense of peace knowing that God is taking care of us, that He has our back, so to speak. I believe that God, while fighting the battle, does expect us to engage. Go back to David. He didn't just stand there and let God hit Goliath with the rock. He took action, using the Lord's strength. He looked his giant square in the eyes, declared victory through God, and whoosh! He let loose with the rock and down went Goliath. David gave glory to God. Would he have been victorious on his own? NO! And he knew it. But we do have an adversary in Satan. He wants nothing more than to take us down, separate us from Jesus, and neutralize us in the battle. But there are some important things to remember as we engage. We have the Lord of lords and King of kings!

"You are of God, little children, and have overcome them because He who is in you is greater than he who is in the world." (1 John 4:4) Satan cannot prevail against the Almighty God!

"No temptation has overtaken you except such as is common to man, but God is faithful, Who will not allow you to be tempted beyond what you are able, but with the temptation will also make the way of escape, that you may be able to bear it." (1 Corinthians 10:13) God will always provide a way out of your predicament. But you need to call on Him before you get in too deep.

"And he said, 'Listen, all you of Judah and you inhabitants of Jerusalem, and you, King Jehoshaphat! Thus says the Lord to you: Do not be afraid nor dismayed because of this great multitude, for the battle is not yours, but God's.'" (2 Chronicles 20:15) In this passage the enemies were preparing to come upon the land. But what did God remind them? The battle was His. We need to remember that as well!

So what are your duties here?
First and foremost, seek the Lord. Go to Him with a humble and contrite heart. If there is sin involved, then you need to confess it to Him and ask for forgiveness.

Secondly, lay it all out. He knows the whole story anyway. No need to hold back! Share every fear and concern with Him.

Thirdly, ask Him to reveal, in His Word, passages that apply to your situation. And to show you what He wants you to do.

Finally, take a deep breath, and trust that He is God. Know, like David did, that God has you covered!

"Be still, and know that I am God; I will be exalted among the nations, I will be exalted in the earth!" (Psalm 46:10)

"The Lord is my light and my salvation; whom shall I fear? The Lord is the strength of my life; of whom shall I be afraid?" (Psalm 27:1) God is our light-He is holy, righteous, and full of grace. He is our salvation-He will save us. He is our strength-through Him we can face anything. We do not need to fear when God is on our side.

"For though we walk in the flesh, we do not war according to the flesh. For the weapons of our warfare are not carnal but mighty in God for pulling down strongholds, casting down arguments and every high thing that exalts itself against the knowledge of God, bringing every thought into captivity to the obedience of Christ" (2 Corinthians 10:3-5) A considerable amount of our battles begin in our hearts and minds. It is vital that we capture these thoughts and cast them aside. We cannot let the enemy get a foothold in the battle.

"Put on the whole armor of God, that you may be able to stand against the wiles of the devil." (Ephesians 6:11). You have to dress for the occasion, right?

So take heart, dear ones. It doesn't matter the size of the giant. God is greater than any of them. There is no doubt about God's ability. The question is, do you believe it when you are in the storm? Can you say it is well with your soul when all is swirling around you like a tornado?

David didn't even question for a moment God's ability to slay Goliath. He trusted in the weapons of our heavenly Father over the handmade weapons of the enemy. Caleb and Joshua trusted in the protection of God. From a shepherd boy to seasoned warriors, the theme was the same. Our God is greater than our surroundings, He is mightier than the enemy before us. He will go before us and fight our battle. Are you willing to let Him do that?

"Yea, though I walk through the valley of the shadow of death, I will fear no evil; for You are with me; Your rod and Your staff, they comfort me." (Psalm 23:4)

BIBLE STUDY AND JOURNAL TIME

Grab your bible, and dig into the chapter's scriptures! Don't forget to read the entire chapter to get the context. And record what the Lord has revealed to you in each passage. Pray for revelation before you begin.

1 SAMUEL 17:45 ("Anchor" passage)

_____
_____
_____
_____
_____
_____
_____
_____

NUMBERS 13:32-33

_____
_____
_____
_____
_____
_____
_____

NUMBERS 14:7-9

_____
_____
_____
_____
_____
_____

1 SAMUEL 17:47

_____
_____
_____
_____
_____
_____
_____
_____
_____

DEUTERONOMY 20:4

_____
_____
_____
_____
_____
_____
_____
_____

DEUTERONOMY 3:22

_____
_____
_____
_____
_____
_____
_____
_____

1 JOHN 4:4

_____

_____

_____

_____

_____

_____

_____

_____

1 CORINTHIANS 10:13

_____

_____

_____

_____

_____

_____

_____

2 CHRONICLES 20:15

_____

_____

_____

_____

_____

_____

_____

_____

PSALM 46:10

_____
_____
_____
_____
_____
_____
_____
_____
_____

PSALM 27:1

_____
_____
_____
_____
_____
_____
_____
_____

2 CORINTHIANS 16:3-5

_____
_____
_____
_____
_____
_____
_____
_____

EPHESIANS 6:11

_____
_____
_____
_____
_____
_____
_____
_____
_____

PSALM 23:4

_____
_____
_____
_____
_____
_____
_____
_____
_____
_____

Now, summarize below what you have learned through the passages. Look for a common theme.

_____

_____

_____

_____

_____

_____

_____

_____

_____

_____

_____

_____

_____

_____

_____

_____

_____

_____

_____

_____

_____

_____

_____

_____

_____

_____

_____

_____

_____

REFLECTION TIME

Think about a giant you have had to face at some point in your life. How did you feel as it loomed before you?

_____
_____
_____
_____
_____

Now that you are familiar with some Bible examples of true warriors, how does your perspective change about your situation?

_____
_____
_____
_____
_____
_____

Meditate on the opening passage about David's response to Goliath. Can you see yourself standing as he did? Put yourself in his sandals. How does that give you confidence to fight your own giants?

_____
_____
_____
_____
_____
_____

Write a prayer asking God to show You His strength when you need it, and to reveal to You passages that you can cling to in times of trials.

_____
_____
_____
_____
_____
_____

Dear Father,

Our days seem to be filled with giants. They appear so overwhelming sometimes. But we know that You are bigger than the giants we face. We thank You that You equip us to be overcomers, to have courage in the battle, and to be victorious because You are with us. Please guide and protect us. Help us to have complete faith and trust in You, our Strength and Protector. In Your Holy name, Amen!

CALL TO ACTION!

Reflect on the story of Caleb and Joshua going back to Numbers 13, where the spies went out. Study the contrast between the spies being fearful of the giants to the point they wanted to run from the potential battle and the confidence of Joshua and Caleb.

Using Joshua and Caleb's response to the situation, think about how having courage in the Lord's ability can overcome the trial ahead of them.

Apply that to a trial you are currently facing. How can seeing God as your strength and protection help you defeat your giant?

Write all your thoughts in your journal.

READY, SET, GO!

In the remaining chapters, we are going to study all the things that Jesus is in our lives. Whatever our need, He is the answer.

CHAPTER 4

HE IS OUR PEACE IN THE STORM

"Now may the Lord of peace Himself give you peace always in every way. The Lord be with you all." (2 Thessalonians 3:16)

I HAVE A PICTURE ON my wall of a beautiful snow-covered field with a large tree and a wood fence. It looks so peaceful I can almost hear the quiet.

Unfortunately, life isn't like that. It feels like we are constantly bombarded by noise, activity, strife, and struggles. Peace is elusive. I am reminded of that old commercial where the gal is at her wit's end. She cries, "Calgon, take me away!" And then she sinks into a bathtub full of bubbles. All is right in her world again, at least for the moment. Wouldn't that be nice if we could escape the chaos? Jesus gives us a way:

"Peace I leave with you, My peace I give to you; not as the world gives do I give to you. Let not your heart be troubled, neither let it be afraid." (John 14:27) There is nothing like the peace that comes from the comforting hand of our Lord Jesus!

"Now may the God of hope fill you with all joy and peace in believing, that you may abound in hope by the power of the Holy Spirit." (Romans 15:13)

What is peace, anyway? The dictionary describes it as a time of "non-war" between nations. It has been called a lack of conflict. Harmony between neighbors. Absence of noise and confusion. Calm or quiet, "the peace before the storm." But here, we want to look deeper than outer circumstances. As always, we look at the heart.

Oftentimes, I feel a restlessness in my soul. There is a struggle between what decision I need to make. There is worry or fear about an upcoming situation. Or maybe I am battling with an unresolved issue with a friend or family member. Any one of these situations can cause an unsettledness in my heart, keeping peace at a distance.

WHAT ROBS US OF OUR PEACE?

FEAR

I am reminded of the story in Mark 4:35-41. Jesus had spent the day teaching the multitudes by the sea of Galilee. When the day was done, this happened:

"On the same day, when evening had come, He said to them, 'Let us cross over to the other side.' Now when they had left the multitude, they took Him along in the boat as He was. And other little boats were also with Him. And a great windstorm arose, and the waves beat into the boat so that it was already filling. But He was in the stern, asleep on a pillow. And they awoke Him and said to Him, 'Teacher, do You not care that we are perishing?'

Then He arose and rebuked the wind, and said to the sea, 'Peace, be still!' And the wind ceased and there was a great calm. But He said to them, 'Why are you so fearful? How is it that you have no faith?' And they feared exceedingly, and said to one another, 'Who can this be, that even the wind and the sea obey Him!'"

In this passage, we see a contrast between man's natural fear in a potentially dangerous situation and our Savior, who is at total peace. Why were these men afraid? Afterall, they were seasoned fishermen. No doubt they had experienced bad storms many, many times. Maybe it was the darkness. Things tend to look worse at night than they do in the light of day. Or maybe it was the suddenness and severity of the storm. The scripture doesn't say. But their fearless leader, Jesus, was just that-fearless. Back in the boat, He was taking a snooze while doom and disaster were knocking at the door. I'm sure we have all had that experience where a tidal wave is crashing upon us. We are in total panic mode, then someone comes along and says essentially, "What's the problem? This is no big deal." It feels like nobody cares about your struggle. They just go merrily along with their life and ignore your turmoil. That's how these guys felt. "Don't you care that we are going down?"

I like the simple act of Jesus. He rebukes the wind and waves and then rebukes the nonbelievers. Wouldn't you love to have that peace and calm in your heart when in a storm? You can if you just look to the Peace-giver.

"You will keep him in perfect peace, whose mind is stayed on You, because he trusts in You." (Isaiah 26:3) There is some action required from us if we want to experience the peace He has promised. We need to keep our focus on Him, and fully trust Him no matter what.

"I will both lie down in peace, and sleep; for You alone, O Lord, make me dwell in safety." (Psalm 4:8) Problems have a way of taking on a life of their own when we close our eyes to sleep. But Jesus provides the peace that we need to let go of the issues that are so pressing.

"And let the peace of God rule in your hearts, to which also you were called in one body; and be thankful." (Colossians 3:15) There is a continuous battle in our hearts. The enemy wants to see us in constant turmoil, wrestling over issues, being at odds with our Lord. Satan knows that if we are fearful, anxious, and in a state of stress and panic, there is no room for God to rule in our hearts. We can only serve one master, and we don't want it to be the evil one, right?

ANXIETY

"Be anxious for nothing, but in everything by prayer and supplication, with thanksgiving, let your requests be made known to God; and the peace of God, which surpasses all understanding, will guard your hearts and minds through Christ Jesus." (Philippians 4:6-7). Have you ever experienced that peace that comes into your heart that you just can't understand? You're thinking, "I should be really upset about this, but there is a calmness in my soul that I can't explain." The world around you may be spinning out of control, but you can honestly say, "It is well with my soul". It certainly confounds those near you!

"Therefore do not worry about tomorrow, for tomorrow will worry about its own things. Sufficient for the day is its own trouble."

(Matthew 6:34) Do you find yourself worrying about things down the road that you have no control over, that might not even happen? We need to keep our eyes on today. That should keep us occupied!

"For God has not given us a spirit of fear, but of power and of love and of a sound mind." (2 Timothy 1:7) Fear does NOT come from God; it comes from the enemy. Claim the Power. Then Satan has to flee.

CONFLICT
This can rear its ugly head so easily between one another, or even within ourselves. But God does not want us to strive with this issue. And of course, He gives us tools to combat it:

"Pursue peace with all people, and holiness, without which no one will see the Lord." (Hebrews 12:14) The key to this, I think, is grace upon grace, dying to ourselves, and putting others above us.

"And be kind to one another, tenderhearted, forgiving one another, even as God in Christ forgave you." (Ephesians 4:32) Unforgiveness can eat at our souls like cancer. Whether it be an issue with someone else or that inner struggle with our own conscience. Forgiveness, forgiveness, forgiveness! It goes a long way in slaying that giant!

"For the flesh lusts against the Spirit, and the Spirit against the flesh; and these are contrary to one another, so that you do not do the things that you wish." (Galatians 5:17) Oh, the Spirit is willing, but the flesh is weak! The battle is relentless. When we give into our flesh, the enemy is right there taunting us, making us feel even worse. Save yourself the grief and make no provision for it. When you are struggling with a temptation, cry out to the Lord for victory!

To obtain true peace, we need to stop searching for it in the world. Because it is fleeting. And it requires the absence of strife. Good luck with that in this day and age! The true peace that comes from Jesus transcends turmoil, trials, fears, or anything that man tries to use to achieve it. Seek Him diligently when you are anxious or fearful. He will calm every storm.

"Casting all your care upon Him, for He cares for you." (1 Peter 5:7)

BIBLE STUDY AND JOURNAL TIME

Grab your bible, and dig into the chapter's scriptures! Don't forget to read the entire chapter to get the context. And record what the Lord has revealed to you in each passage. Pray for revelation before you begin.

2 THESSALONIANS 3:16 ("Anchor" passage)

_____
_____
_____
_____
_____
_____
_____
_____

JOHN 14:27

_____
_____
_____
_____
_____
_____
_____

ROMANS 15:13

_____
_____
_____
_____
_____
_____

MARK 4:35-41

_____
_____
_____
_____
_____
_____
_____
_____
_____

ISAIAH 26:3

_____
_____
_____
_____
_____
_____
_____
_____

PSALM 4:8

_____
_____
_____
_____
_____
_____
_____
_____
_____

COLOSSIANS 3:15

_____
_____
_____
_____
_____
_____
_____
_____
_____

PHILIPPIANS 4:6-7

_____
_____
_____
_____
_____
_____
_____
_____

MATTHEW 6:34-41

_____
_____
_____
_____
_____
_____
_____
_____

2 TIMOTHY 1:7

_____

_____

_____

_____

_____

_____

_____

_____

_____

HEBREWS 12:14

_____

_____

_____

_____

_____

_____

_____

_____

EPHESIANS 4:32

_____

_____

_____

_____

_____

_____

_____

_____

_____

GALATIANS 5:17

_____
_____
_____
_____
_____
_____
_____
_____
_____

1 PETER 5:7

_____
_____
_____
_____
_____
_____
_____
_____
_____

Now, summarize below what you have learned through the passages. Look for a common theme.

_____

_____

_____

_____

_____

_____

_____

_____

_____

_____

_____

_____

_____

_____

_____

_____

_____

_____

_____

_____

_____

_____

_____

_____

_____

_____

_____

_____

_____

_____

_____

_____

_____

_____

REFLECTION TIME

What are some things that are preventing you from having peace in your heart?

_____

_____

_____

_____

_____

Now that you have identified them, which scriptures in this chapter give you comfort in conquering them?

_____

_____

_____

_____

_____

_____

Meditate on the opening passage about finding peace with God. Are you able to keep your mind stayed upon Him, or do you find yourself bouncing back into the "what-if" mode?

_____

_____

_____

_____

_____

_____

Write a prayer asking God to help you keep your mind stayed on Him, and to guard against fearful and worrisome thoughts.

_____

_____

_____

_____

_____

_____

Dear Heavenly Father:

Thank You that You are not the author of confusion, but the God of peace, comfort, and order. It is so easy to allow ourselves to let fearful or anxious thoughts take hold in our minds. Help us to immediately take captive of these, give them to You, and be able to enjoy the peace that can come only from You.

In Your Name, Amen!

CALL TO ACTION

Take a look at the scriptures we studied in this chapter. Commit to memorizing at least three of these that you can use to call on the Lord, and to help you defeat the enemy's efforts to keep you from peace in your heart. Flashcards work really well for this exercise. Post them around your house, or in your car, or bible, somewhere where they will be visible.

READY, SET, GO!

CHAPTER 5

HE IS OUR STRENGTH IN TIMES OF WEAKNESS

"He gives power to the weak, and to those who have no might He increases strength. Even the youths shall faint and be weary, and the young men shall utterly fall. But those who wait on the LORD shall renew their strength; they shall mount up with wings like eagles, they shall run and not be weary, they shall walk and not faint." (Isaiah 40:29-31)

THIS IS ONE OF MY favorite passages in the Bible. First of all, I love to watch an eagle soaring through the air. They have this wonderful sense of majesty and power. They are incredibly strong; they can snatch away little Fluffy or Fido with ease (sorry for that image!). An interesting tidbit I discovered in my research here. They don't eat dead stuff! They like fresh meat. Feel free to put whatever spiritual spin on that you want.

Getting back to our scripture. Have you ever felt bone-weary, drained of every drop of energy, feeling like you can't go another step? I think we all have been in that moment. It might be physical fatigue, or it might be that the weight of the world is on your shoulders. Walking another step seems impossible, never mind running.

But we are so incredibly blessed that we have a Savior who can renew and refresh us, carry our load, and strengthen our weary bones. If we wait on Him, He will lift us up. He will give us the courage and fortitude to face the battles of life.

So often when we are weak, we fail to call out to the Strength-giver. Some passages to consider when you feel you can't go another step:

"The Lord is my strength and song, and He has become my salvation; He is my God, and I will praise Him; my father's God, and I will exalt Him." (Exodus 15:2) Singing praises to the Lord in difficult situations can give us that renewed strength that we need. Music in the heart is an elixir for the soul!

"Do not sorrow, for the joy of the Lord is your strength." (Nehemiah 8:10b) When we are going through painful times, rejoicing in the Lord will help get our minds off our circumstances and give us a sense of peace.

"God is our refuge and strength, a very present help in trouble." (Psalm 46:1) When we are in crisis mode, calling out to the Living God for His help will give us shelter in that storm and the strength to endure it.

"My soul melts from heaviness; strengthen me according to Your Word." (Psalm 119:28) Have you ever felt like you were melting into a puddle from fatigue and worry? Dig into His word and let it give you strength and hope.

"Not that I speak in regard to need, for I have learned in whatever state I am, to be content: I know how to be abased, and I know how to abound. Everywhere and in all things I have learned both to be full and to be hungry, both to abound and to suffer need. I can do all things through Christ who strengthens me." (Philippians 4:11-13) If anyone can speak about trials, Paul can. He had suffered multitudes of them. Yet because of his love for Jesus, he knew that he could be content in any situation if he stayed close to Him.

"And let us not grow weary while doing good, for in due season we shall reap if we do not lose heart." (Galatians 6:9) Sometimes it feels like no matter what we do or how long we toil, we don't see the fruits of our labors. But if we stay strong in Christ, the harvest will come!

"The Lord is my strength and my shield; my heart trusted in Him, and I am helped; therefore my heart greatly rejoices, and with my song I will praise Him." (Psalm 28:7) The Word of God is powerful, His promises are true. We can rejoice in His faithfulness, His protection, and

His strength. That's worth a praise song or two! But you might be thinking "I'm not sure how to draw on His strength. Where do I begin?"

"Seek the Lord and His strength; seek His face evermore!" (1 Chronicles 16:11) We need to constantly press into Him, study His Word, and draw our strength from Him. We can't do it in our own strength.

"Ah, Lord God! Behold, You have made the heavens and the earth by Your great power and outstretched arm. There is nothing too hard for You." (Jeremiah 32:17) I don't understand why we think that the Creator of the universe, who holds the stars in His hands, who gives us the very breath of life can't solve our issues or see us through our trial. But we do that, don't we? Oh, maybe not consciously, but sometimes it is hard to put our trust and faith in something unseen. We feel better if our help is tangible.

"Have I not commanded you? Be strong and of good courage; do not be afraid, nor be dismayed, for the Lord your God is with you wherever you go." (Joshua 1:9) Joshua was given this command three times in the first chapter. To be honest, if somebody sent me out to do something, and repeatedly told me not to be afraid, I think I might be wondering what was going to happen that I would need to be told that so often.

God will always prepare us for the battle ahead. He will supply everything we need, especially strength for the journey. We have nothing to fear because He promises to be with us. That doesn't guarantee a smooth ride, not by a long shot. All you have to do is look at the life of Paul. He suffered a lot for being an ambassador of Christ. But he knew that the prize would be worth every beating, shipwreck, and imprisonment. I don't think he would have given up any one of those trials if it meant that he would not see Jesus when his race was finished.

"My flesh and my heart fail, but God is the strength of my heart and my portion forever." (Psalm 73:26) As we run this race of life, it can feel much like a marathon race. The marathoner may reach a point that's called the "wall". This is where the runner, even though he has trained for a long time, feels he cannot go another step. His body has been depleted of all its

stored glycogen. Then he is hit with total physical and mental exhaustion. He can hardly move, and his brain seems to stop working. This happens around the twenty-mile mark. Interestingly, one of the ways to push through the wall, as experts suggest, is to have a friend with you to encourage you through it. I would say that there is no better Person to encourage and strengthen us through the truly hard times than Jesus! Call on His name, and sing praises to Him. Recite scripture. PRAY! Connect any way you can and you will find yourself energized and feeling victorious again!

"And lest I should be exalted above measure by the abundance of the revelations, a thorn in the flesh was given to me, a messenger of Satan to buffet me, lest I be exalted above measure. Concerning this thing I pleaded with the Lord three times that it might depart from me. And He said to me, 'My grace is sufficient for you, for My strength is made perfect in weakness.' Therefore most gladly I will rather boast in my infirmities, that the power of Christ may rest upon me. Therefore I take pleasure in infirmities, in reproaches, in needs, in persecutions, in distresses, for Christ's sake. For when I am weak, then I am strong." (2 Corinthians 12:7-10) As mentioned before, Paul had more than his share of trials. And he was only human. He was suffering through a particularly challenging one. He pleaded with the Lord to remove it. But God said "No." He wasn't being cruel in denying Paul's fervent plea. He was using it to refine, to grow, to keep him humble maybe. The trial wasn't wasted on him. Through it, he realized that God would manifest Himself and work powerfully through his infirmity. So instead of moaning about his situation, Paul learned, drew upon, and ultimately boasted about how Jesus worked amazing things in and through him.

May I encourage you to look for Jesus for that supernatural strength when you are weak or weary? He is the Strength-giver, the Energizer, the Power in us. He will give us what we need to get through the storm, and we will be victorious in and through whatever comes our way!

"The Lord will give strength to His people; the Lord will bless His people with peace." (Psalm 29:11)

56

BIBLE STUDY AND JOURNAL TIME

Grab your bible, and dig into the chapter's scriptures! Don't forget to read the entire chapter to get the context. And record what the Lord has revealed to you in each passage. Pray for revelation before you begin.

ISAIAH 40:29-31 ("Anchor" passage)

_____
_____
_____
_____
_____
_____
_____
_____

EXODUS 15:2

_____
_____
_____
_____
_____
_____
_____

NEHEMIAH 8:10B

_____
_____
_____
_____
_____
_____

PSALM 46:1-5

_____

_____

_____

_____

_____

_____

_____

_____

_____

_____

PSALM 119:20

_____

_____

_____

_____

_____

_____

_____

_____

PHILIPPIANS 4:11-13

_____

_____

_____

_____

_____

_____

_____

_____

GALATIANS 6:9

_____
_____
_____
_____
_____
_____
_____
_____
_____
_____

PSALM 28:7

_____
_____
_____
_____
_____
_____
_____
_____

1 CHRONICLES 16:11

_____
_____
_____
_____
_____
_____
_____
_____

JEREMIAH 32:17

_____
_____
_____
_____
_____
_____
_____
_____
_____
_____

JOSHUA 1:9

_____
_____
_____
_____
_____
_____
_____
_____
_____

PSALM 72:26

_____
_____
_____
_____
_____
_____
_____
_____
_____

2 CORINTHIANS 12:7-10

_____
_____
_____
_____
_____
_____
_____
_____
_____
_____

PSALM 29:11

_____
_____
_____
_____
_____
_____
_____
_____
_____
_____

Now, summarize below what you have learned through the passages. Look for a common theme.

_____

_____

_____

_____

_____

_____

_____

_____

_____

_____

_____

_____

_____

_____

_____

_____

_____

_____

_____

_____

_____

_____

_____

_____

_____

_____

_____

_____

_____

_____

_____

_____

REFLECTION TIME

Take a look at our anchor passage (Isaiah 40:29-31). Have you ever been so weary that you felt you were going to collapse right then and there? How would this passage give you the strength you needed to carry on?

_____

_____

_____

_____

_____

Have you ever felt His supernatural strength? Describe the transformation you experienced.

_____

_____

_____

_____

_____

Review the scriptures in this chapter. Which one resonates with you and why

_____

_____

_____

_____

_____

_____

Write out a prayer asking God to give you strength when you are weary, and to give you courage to continue to carry out what He asked of you.

_____

_____

_____

_____

_____

Thank You Jesus that You are my strength and my song. An ever present help in times of trouble. Thank You that I can cry out to You in times of weakness, and trust that You will give me the strength to face one more day, one more moment. This world can wear us down and beat us up. But You are there, ready to lift us up on eagles wings, to raise us up above the swirling waters. That knowledge is so comforting. Thank You! In Your Precious Name, Amen

CALL TO ACTION

Okay, we are going to tax those little gray cells again. Review all the scriptures in this chapter. Choose three that speak to your heart and commit them to memory. We want to have an arsenal in our memory banks that we can call on when the difficulties arise. Write them on post-it notes and put them on the fridge, in your bible, your lunchbox. Put them wherever you will see them and be reminded of them.

READY, SET, GO!

CHAPTER 6

HE IS OUR HOPE WHEN ALL SEEMS LOST

"This hope we have as an anchor of the soul, both sure and steadfast, and which enters the Presence behind the veil." (Hebrews 6:19)

HOPE, ACCORDING TO THE DICTIONARY, is a state of uncertain expectation. I hope I get that new job. I hope he asks me to the prom. I hope they know what they are talking about. There is a level of desire attached, but not something we can put our total trust in.

Hope often creates unrealistic expectations. I remember years ago, I wanted to work for a certain company. It looked like the perfect fit. It was a retail store, right up my alley. But when I got in there, it was a nightmare from day one. I couldn't believe it! I hung in there for three months. Another time, I was offered a position with a start-up company that was still in the development stage. I had several wonderful conversations with the owner; we were on the same page in every aspect. This went on for about a year, as she kept having delays in getting it started. But when it came close to fruition, we had a meeting. I walked away from there with such a knot in my stomach. This wasn't going to be what I thought. And to my amazement, after investing over a year of hope, I walked away from the opportunity. Looking back, I thank the Lord for protecting me from getting involved. I believe the business went under after a couple of years. I also heard through the grapevine that she was very difficult to work with. No thanks!

My expectations in both these situations were based on earthly plans. I was expecting them to be a certain way, and both fell short. But hope in God's economy is an entirely different thing. Biblical hope is a certainty steeped in an unchanging, unfailing Savior. As our "anchor" scripture for this chapter states, hope is the anchor of our souls. Jesus keeps us grounded and solid, not miring in fragile desires and shaky outcomes. We are buffeted from the slings and arrows by His loving arms around us.

The hope of Jesus is rock solid. Just like an anchor keeps a boat steady from wind and turbulence, our hope in Jesus keeps us from being tossed to and fro in the storms of life. We are securely tethered to Him.

"Now faith is the substance of things hoped for, the evidence of things not seen." (Hebrews 11:1) So what is biblical hope? It is a firm assurance that we have even in uncertain situations. It doesn't depend on a positive outcome. It is rooted in our faith in the resurrected Jesus. It won't diminish when things don't go as we wanted. Why? Because this hope is not tied to earthly expectations. We know that God is faithful. We believe that our salvation is sure, and we look forward with anticipation to eternity with Him. We believe in His Word, that His promises are true, and we believe in the power of the Holy Spirit.

"Let us hold fast the confession of our hope without wavering, for He who promised is faithful" (Hebrews 10:23) When we put our complete trust and faith in Jesus Christ, He is faithful in every aspect of our life. He doesn't promise we will get everything we want, but He will certainly provide us with everything we need.

"For we were saved in this hope, but hope that is seen is not hope; for why does one still hope for what he sees? But if we hope for what we do not see, we eagerly wait for it with perseverance." (Romans 8:24-25) When we were first saved, we weren't given the full complement of our benefits. The greatest thing promised that we cannot see now is the glorious future in heaven and eternity with our Savior.! That is something we can definitely put our hope in!

"Blessed be the God and Father of our Lord Jesus, who according to His abundant mercy has begotten us again to a living hope through the resurrection of Jesus Christ from the dead." (1 Peter 1:3) When Jesus died on the cross, the penalty of all our past and future sins was paid.

Without it, we would not have salvation, But it was through His glorious resurrection that we have been declared righteous. We are free of sin and death. And because He lives, so will we.

If you will remember when Jesus took all the sins of the world upon Him while on the cross, the Father had to look away. He could not look upon sin. So it is with us. If we were still in our sins, we could not be in the presence of the Holy One. But the death of Jesus on the cross and His resurrection tore that veil that separated us. Hallelujah!

You might be thinking right now that all sounds wonderful, I believe it and can hardly wait. But what about now, in this present time? How can having hope help me through this trial I am in today?

Hope gives us strength. It gives us peace. It helps us to put the burden on the only One who can truly see us through the troubled waters. It gives us patience and endurance.

"Behold, the eye of the Lord is on those who fear Him, on those who hope in His mercy," (Psalm 33:18) There are probably times when we feel there is no way out. We may even feel abandoned by Him. But trust His Word. His eye is on us, and He will have mercy on us. Then, look what happens:

"The eyes of your understanding being enlightened; that you may know what is the hope of His calling, what are the riches of the glory of His inheritance in the saints" (Ephesians 1:18) When you hold onto the hope of Jesus, you will have an entire new perspective of His love and care for you.

"To them God willed to make known what are the riches of the glory of this mystery among the Gentiles: which is Christ in you, the hope of glory." (Colossians 1:27) The mystery revolved around the fact that God would be willing to make the Gentiles fellow heirs. His love went beyond the Abrahamic covenant. He dwells in any heart that receives Him as Lord and Savior. We all share the same hope of eternal glory. There is no longer Jew or Gentile.

"For the needy shall not always be forgotten; the expectation (hope) of the poor shall not perish forever." (Psalm 9:18) Sometimes it does feel like we have been forgotten by God. But no matter what we are facing, we can still have that hope, trust, and faith In Him. He hasn't abandoned you. He promises He will never leave you. Hold on tight to that.

"I wait for the Lord, my soul waits, and in His word I do hope." (Psalm 130:5) Our soul and spirit cry out to the living God. And we wait in expectation for Him to show Himself strong in our lives.

"Now hope does not disappoint, because the love of God has been poured out in our hearts by the Holy Spirit who was given to us." (Romans 5:5) Worldly hope disappoints all the time. Our expectations get dashed. And it is especially difficult to deal with when we are let down by a friend or family member. But the hope here is our salvation, poured into us by the indwelling of the Holy Spirit. And it is through God's love for us that this happens.

"But I will hope continually, and will praise You yet more and more." (Psalm 71:14) The psalmist here has begun to overcome his fear of his enemy and comes to the realization that his hope lies in God. His praise will rise higher and higher, and his hope is strengthened. When you are feeling on the brink of defeat, cry out to the Lord and blow the trumpet of praise. You will be refreshed and renewed.

"Let Your mercy, O Lord, be upon us, just as we hope in You." (Psalm 33:22) We all desire the mercy of the Lord. And He has graciously lavished it upon us. We don't deserve it, but we gladly receive it. May it strengthen our hope and trust in Jesus!

When you feel hopeless and defeated, may I encourage you to take your eyes off the situation, and lift your gaze to heaven? Fill your heart with songs of praise for Him. Trust and rest in His promises. May the God of hope fill you with all peace.

"The LORD takes pleasure in those who fear Him, in those who hope in His mercy." (Psalm 147:11)

BIBLE STUDY AND JOURNAL TIME

Grab your bible, and dig into the chapter's scriptures! Don't forget to read the entire chapter to get the context. And record what the Lord has revealed to you in each passage. Pray for revelation before you begin.

HEBREWS 6:19 ("Anchor" passage)

_____
_____
_____
_____
_____
_____
_____
_____
_____

HEBREWS 11:1

_____
_____
_____
_____
_____
_____
_____
_____

HEBREWS 10:23

_____
_____
_____
_____
_____
_____
_____

ROMANS 8:24-25

_____
_____
_____
_____
_____
_____
_____
_____
_____

1 PETER 1:3

_____
_____
_____
_____
_____
_____
_____
_____

PSALM 33:18

_____
_____
_____
_____
_____
_____
_____
_____

EPHESIANS 1:18

_____
_____
_____
_____
_____
_____
_____
_____
_____

COLOSSIANS 1:27

_____
_____
_____
_____
_____
_____
_____
_____

PSALM 9:18

_____
_____
_____
_____
_____
_____
_____
_____

PSALM 130:5

_____
_____
_____
_____
_____
_____
_____
_____
_____

ROMANS 5:5

_____
_____
_____
_____
_____
_____
_____
_____

PSALM 71:14

_____
_____
_____
_____
_____
_____
_____
_____

PSALM 33:22

_____
_____
_____
_____
_____
_____
_____
_____
_____

PSALM 147:11

_____
_____
_____
_____
_____
_____
_____
_____
_____

Now, summarize below what you have learned through the passages. Look for a common theme.

_____
_____
_____
_____
_____
_____
_____
_____
_____
_____
_____
_____
_____
_____
_____
_____
_____
_____
_____
_____
_____
_____
_____
_____
_____
_____
_____
_____
_____
_____

REFLECTION TIME

Think of a time when you had high expectations for something and was disappointed. How would having the hope of Jesus deflect that and help you through it easier?

_____
_____
_____
_____
_____

After studying the passages in this chapter compare and contrast the hope that the world gives and the hope that Jesus gives. Record your thoughts here.

_____
_____
_____
_____
_____

Select one or two of our bible verses that resonate in your heart. Discuss how they impact you.

_____
_____
_____
_____
_____

Write out a prayer thanking God for the hope that He gives us. Ask Him to keep you mindful of this in times of uncertainty.

_____
_____
_____
_____
_____

Dear Heavenly Father: We thank You and praise You for the God that You are. Thank You for making a way through the sacrifice of Your Son that we may have hope for an eternal future with You. Please remind us when we get caught up in our worldly desires and hopes that You are the only One who truly satisfies. We love You and we give You all the glory. Amen!

CALL TO ACTION

A great exercise in learning and applying scripture to our lives is to take a passage and write it out as a prayer, a praise, or to personalize it. So that is your assignment. Take each passage, yes all fourteen, and do just that in your journal.

READY, SET, GO!

CHAPTER 7

HE IS OUR PROVIDER IN TIMES OF NEED

"And my God shall supply all your need according to His riches in glory by Christ Jesus." (Philippians 4:19)

WE CURRENTLY LIVE IN A world where, let's face it, our economy stinks. The rising grocery, gas, and medical costs, plus out-of-control government spending are all causing a financial disaster. To make matters worse, we often live outside our means, purchasing extravagant items that we can't afford in order to feed the beast, which is our flesh. Mortgages, loans, and credit cards are the bane of our existence. Do you remember the recent housing market explosion? People spent hundreds of thousands of dollars over the asking price to outbid everyone and get their dream house that they couldn't afford. Good luck trying to unload it down the road! And every bill comes with a rate increase.

It's scary times, especially if you are living paycheck to paycheck. There is only so much to go around. You can't squeeze blood from a turnip, the old saying goes. But what if I told you that we have a Savior who cares about your practical needs? Who wants to bless you and your family? Would you believe me? Could you hold onto that promise in the dark of night? Let's explore some passages that speak of our great Provider, Jesus.

"Therefore do not worry, saying, 'What shall we eat?' or 'What shall we drink?' or 'What shall we wear?' For after all these things the Gentiles seek. For your heavenly Father knows that you need all these things." (Matthew 6:31) God already knows what we need before we

do. And since He is the Great Provider, we don't need to worry. We need to trust!

"Consider the ravens, for they neither sow nor reap, which have neither storehouse nor barn; and God feeds them. Of how much more value are you than the birds?" (Luke 12:24) Have you ever had the thought, "God doesn't love me. He doesn't care about me." Nothing could be further from the truth! He cares for every living thing, even the birds. And we are far more valuable than a crow! We are fearfully and wonderfully made in His image. "That may be all well and good," you might say. "It's a long way from knowing He cares about me and seeing my needs met."

One of the key things to having our Heavenly Father provide for us is to recognize the difference between what we need and what we want. Oh, the flesh likes to raise its ugly head, dangling that latest iPhone version, the super cute shoes you can't live without, or the expensive restaurant way above your budget. That familiar rationale pops up, "I deserve it. I've worked hard." And you may lessen, or at least postpone, the guilt by whipping out the charge card. Defer the pain.

God is clear that although He loves us and wants the best for us, He wants us to recognize what is really important. So what does that mean in our opening verse, "God will supply all your need"? Don't miss the word "according". It is His economy, not ours. He wants us to be good stewards of what He has already given us. If we are squandering money and then not be able to pay our bills, He isn't going to reward our irresponsibility. God wants us to be faithful with what He has given us.

"And whatever things you ask in prayer, believing, you will receive." (Matthew 21:22) It is important to remember that there is more than just asking for whatever we want, and by believing, we will receive it. We are to ask according to His will. God is not simply an indulgent father, spoiling his kids. Our will needs to be aligned with His. If we are truly seeking Him and seeking to do His will, then our prayers will automatically line up with that, and we will not ask for things that are not good for us.

"Ask, and it will be given to you; seek, and you will find; knock, and it will be opened to you." (Matthew 7:7) Again, we need to be in His will, asking for those things that honor Him. Do we want Him to provide things that are not beneficial? Children ask their parents for their whims in that manner because they haven't developed the ability to properly discern what is good and what is harmful. But when we seek Him, we will develop the spiritual maturity to desire His best for us.

"But seek first the kingdom of God and His righteousness, and all these things shall be added to you." (Matthew 6:33) First and foremost, we need to be always seeking God. We need to put our spiritual needs above our flesh. If we do that, we will be in line with what God has for us, and it will be provided abundantly.

"Every good gift and every perfect gift is from above, and comes down from the Father of lights, with whom there is no variation or shadow of turning." (James 1:17) God will not withhold anything good from us. But we must understand that He will close the door when we ask selfishly for things that ultimately will harm us.

"The young lions lack and suffer hunger, but those who seek the LORD shall not lack any good thing." (Psalm 34:10) Have you ever had to go out and hunt for your food? The grocery store doesn't count! The lion painstakingly seeks his prey, and if he isn't successful, he goes hungry for the day. I believe the hunger here refers to the longing of the soul. If we are spiritually hungry and seeking after Him, He will provide exactly what we need.

"For He satisfies the longing soul, and fills the hungry soul with goodness." (Psalm 107:9) Sometimes we are searching elusively for that one thing that will satisfy. But Jesus will fill that void every time.

"If you then, being evil, know how to give good gifts to your children, how much more will your Father who is in heaven give good things to those who ask Him!" (Matthew 7:11) Even in our morally depraved state, we know how to provide for our children. Those good gifts pale in comparison to the riches that flow from heaven.

"Then Abraham lifted his eyes and looked, and there behind him was a ram caught in a thicket by its horns. So Abraham went and took the ram, and offered it up for a burnt offering instead of his son. And Abraham called the name of the place, The-Lord-Will-Provide; as it is said to this day, 'In the Mount of the Lord it shall be provided.'" (Genesis 22:13-14) I love this story. Abraham was tested by God. He was asked to sacrifice his only son. As painful and difficult as this was, Abraham chose to be obedient to God. He was faithful to the calling. God honored it and provided the sacrifice that was needed. Are you willing to sacrifice that which is dear to you if the Lord should ask?

"'Bring all the tithes into the storehouse, that there may be food in My house, and try Me now in this,' says the Lord of hosts, 'If I will not open for you the windows of heaven and pour out for you such blessing that there will not be room enough to receive it.'" (Malachi 3:10) This is the only place in the Bible where God asks us to test Him. We hold onto our money as if it was a lifeline. It can be scary to let go when you are already scrimping and saving to get by. After all, your payment on that fancy car is due! But He is challenging us to trust Him.

"Honor the Lord with your possessions, and with the firstfruits of all your increase; so your barns will be filled with plenty, and your vats will overflow with new wine." (Proverbs 3:9-10) I have found that when I choose to honor God with my firstfruits, He is faithful to provide. It doesn't mean that you will wake up tomorrow with a garage full of $100 bills. But He will bless you in ways beyond what you can imagine.

So, the exhortation here is that God will provide everything we need, but He wants us to be making "deposits" into our spiritual bank. Seek Him, serve Him, trust Him, honor Him. Live a life that is pleasing to Him, and you will be amazed at the riches you gain!

"Do not fear, little flock, for it is your Father's good pleasure to give you the kingdom." (Luke 12:32)

BIBLE STUDY AND JOURNAL TIME

Grab your bible, and dig into the chapter's scriptures! Don't forget to read the entire chapter to get the context. And record what the Lord has revealed to you in each passage. Pray for revelation before you begin.

PHILIPPIANS 4:19 ("Anchor" passage)

_____

_____

_____

_____

_____

_____

_____

_____

MATTHEW 6:31

_____

_____

_____

_____

_____

_____

_____

LUKE 12:24

_____

_____

_____

_____

_____

_____

MATTHEW 21:22

_____
_____
_____
_____
_____
_____
_____
_____

MATTHEW 7:7

_____
_____
_____
_____
_____
_____
_____
_____

MATTHEW 6:33

_____
_____
_____
_____
_____
_____
_____
_____

JAMES 1:17

_____
_____
_____
_____
_____
_____
_____
_____
_____

PSALM 34:10

_____
_____
_____
_____
_____
_____
_____
_____

PSALM 107:9

_____
_____
_____
_____
_____
_____
_____
_____

MATTHEW 7:11

GENESIS 22:13-14

MALACHI 3:10

PROVERBS 3:9-10

_____

_____

_____

_____

_____

_____

_____

_____

LUKE 12:32

_____

_____

_____

_____

_____

_____

_____

_____

_____

Now, summarize below what you have learned through the passages. Look for a common theme.

_____
_____
_____
_____
_____
_____
_____
_____
_____
_____
_____
_____
_____
_____
_____
_____
_____
_____
_____
_____
_____
_____
_____
_____
_____
_____
_____
_____
_____
_____

REFLECTION TIME

Do you find yourself worrying about financial provision, or have you in the past? Which scripture studied in this chapter gives you comfort and why?

_____

_____

_____

_____

_____

Think about the things you "need" versus the things you "want". How do they line up with what God promises to provide?

_____

_____

_____

_____

_____

In our verse, Malachi 3:10, God actually challenges us to test His provision when we tithe. Have you found that to be true? If so, how?

_____

_____

_____

_____

_____

Write out a prayer thanking God for all that He has provided you, and to help you to be a good steward of those things. Ask Him to reveal to you how to better ask for what you need (what would line up with His will)

_____

_____

_____

_____

_____

Dear Heavenly Father: Thank You for all of the wonderful gifts You give to Your children. They reveal themselves in so many ways, beyond the tangible. A beautiful sunset, a timely call from a dear friend, the peace we receive when we seek Your comfort. These are priceless beyond measure. But most of all, thank You for the ultimate gift- our very salvation. In Your Name, amen!

CALL TO ACTION

Hopefully, through this chapter's study, you have gained a new perspective on how our heavenly Father provides for us. Here is your assignment, In your journal, make a list of things that you actually need, and things that are maybe just a desire. Focus on the needs, and continue to seek Him for them, praying that His will be done. We don't want "stuff" that just clutters our lives or hearts. Purpose in your heart to let go of the things that weigh you down.

READY, SET, GO!

CHAPTER 8

HE IS OUR PROTECTOR IN TIMES OF DANGER

"He who dwells in the secret place of the Most High shall abide under the shadow of the Almighty. I will say of the Lord, 'He is my refuge and my fortress; my God, in Him I will trust.'" (Psalm 91:1-2)

WHAT A BEAUTIFUL PICTURE OUR scripture for this chapter paints. When I read this passage, I imagine that I am securely wrapped in the loving arms of Jesus, safely tucked away from all harm. I have nothing to fear because He is going to keep me safe.

There are so many things that attack our sense of well-being. Sometimes it is a physical threat. But more often, our insecurity stems from fears of persecution, criticism, financial woes, marriage problems; you name it. Our world can get rocked at any time. And you can bet that the enemy will push all of our buttons when he senses fear. Like a shark in the water smelling blood, he is circling in for the kill.

When we feel threatened, we can respond in a variety of ways. We can freak out. That might make us feel better for a moment, but hardly productive. We can go on the offensive, looking for ways to fight back at our attacker, trying to do things in our own strength. Or we can seek the Lord and His protection. It's easy to lose sight of option #3. We feel we need to do something, anything, to fix the problem. But God is the ultimate problem solver! He is mighty in power, greater than our battles. He wants us to cry out to Him for His protection.

"Be merciful to me, O God, be merciful to me! For my soul trusts in You; and in the shadow of Your wings I will make my refuge until

these calamities have passed by." (Psalm 57:1) Under His wings is the safest place I can think to hide from the slings and arrows coming after me.

"The name of the Lord is a strong tower; the righteous run to it and are safe." (Proverbs 18:10). The righteous, those of us who claim Jesus as our Lord and Savior, have that strong tower to which we can run and find safety that the world cannot provide. There is great power in the name of Jesus. When we are being attacked by the enemy, we need to cry out the name of Jesus and the devil has to flee. He trembles at the name of our Lord.

"But the Lord is faithful, Who will establish you and guard you from the evil one." (2 Thessalonians 3:3) God is faithful in His promises that He will keep us out of the snare of the devil.

"But let all those rejoice who put their trust in You; let them ever shout for joy, because You defend them; let those also who love Your name be joyful in You." (Psalm 5:11) Doesn't your heart want to sing praises to the Lord for His loving protection and defense in our time of need? Next time you feel frightened or worried, shout out a praise or two to Him. Sing your favorite hymn or worship song. Let it fill your heart with joy, and those scary thoughts will be pushed right out of your mind.

"'For the oppression of the poor, for the sighing of the needy, now I will arise,' says the Lord; 'I will set him in the safety for which he yearns.'" (Psalm 12:5) When our physical needs are not being met and we don't see a way out of our troubles, God will provide the very things we need. He cares for the little sparrow, so how much more does He care for us? A lot more!

"May the Lord answer you in the day of trouble; may the name of the God of Jacob defend you." (Psalm 20:1) God will take care of you in the moment that you need it. Let Him be your defense. It will be far more effective than anything we could muster.

"Deliver me from my enemies, O my God; defend me from those who rise up against me." (Psalm 59:1) The Bible says many times that God

is our defense. The enemy will always be on the attack. If we let God fight the battle, we will always be victorious.

"Keep me as the apple of Your eye; hide me under the shadow of Your wings." (Psalm 17:8) When you look into someone's pupil, you can actually see your reflection. The iris is very sensitive and needs to be protected. To be the apple of God's eye is to be a reflection of Him. It also needs to be protected. As His children, we are safeguarded, loved, and sheltered.

"How precious is Your lovingkindness, O God! Therefore the children of men put their trust under the shadow of Your wings." (Psalm 36:7) His lovingkindness is better than life. And what is more precious than that? We know that we are safe in the shadow of His wing because it covers us completely.

"Though I walk in the midst of trouble, You will revive me; You will stretch out Your hand against the wrath of my enemies, and Your right hand will save me." (Psalm 138:7) Battles and struggles can wear us down to the bone. But God will strengthen and renew us. The Lord, our strength and our deliverer, will guard us and keep us safe from the relentless attacks of the enemy. When I read this passage I have a sense of peace and refreshment. I know that He will be surrounding me with His love.

"The Lord is your keeper; the Lord is your shade at your right hand. The sun shall not strike you by day, nor the moon by night." (Psalm 121:5-6) He will guard and protect us morning, noon, and night!

"A thousand may fall at your side, and ten thousand at your right hand; but it shall not come near you. Only with your eyes shall you look and see the reward of the wicked. Because you have made the Lord, who is my refuge, even the Most High, your dwelling place." (Psalm 91:7-9) Having Jesus as my dwelling place is the safest place I can think of to be. When the enemy is attacking from all fronts, and so often it feels that way, God will go before us, behind us, beside us. He is our shield and buckler. If we let Him fight our battles, we will

see the shackles of worry, despair, anger, whatever it may be, fall to the wayside. We will have the vantage point under His wing as we watch the enemy crushed.

So why do we insist on going into battle alone? Why do we try to fight the enemy ourselves, when we have such a powerful advocate in our Lord? We will see a greater victory when we allow God, who is far more powerful than we are, to fight the battle. When David slew Goliath with the rock, don't for a moment think it was the rock that gave him the victory. It was the power and might of our Almighty God!

Now, there may be times when God calls us to fight. But it is not with the armor of the flesh or the world. We go into battle with our spiritual armor on and trust that God is leading the fight. We are just foot soldiers. I don't know about you, but I like the idea of standing in His shadow, with His mighty hand of protection on me. Those slings and arrows are going to bounce right off. He will deflect them with just a touch or a word. No earthly battle, whether it be in my heart or whether it be nation against nation, will ever be resolved like that.

Here's a peek at coming attractions for you: Revelation 19 describes that at the end of the Tribulation period, Jesus will come down (and we get to ride with him!) and finally destroy Satan and his cohorts once and for all. He plants His foot on the Mount of Olives, splitting it in two, and He uses a mighty sword to devour the enemy that has caused so much turmoil. It will be swift and just. He will declare Himself King of kings and Lord of lords. That's exciting to me! And that is the Lord that you and I have ready to fight our battles and protect us from the evil one, right now, today. How can we do better than that? Just remember, He has your back!

The horse is prepared for the day of battle, but deliverance is of the LORD. (Proverbs 21:31)

BIBLE STUDY AND JOURNAL TIME

Grab your bible, and dig into the chapter's scriptures! Don't forget to read the entire chapter to get the context. And record what the Lord has revealed to you in each passage.

PSALM 91:1-2 ("Anchor" passage)

_____

_____

_____

_____

_____

_____

_____

_____

PSALM 57:1

_____

_____

_____

_____

_____

_____

_____

PROVERBS 18:10

_____

_____

_____

_____

_____

_____

_____

2 THESSALONIANS 3:3

_____

_____

_____

_____

_____

_____

_____

_____

PSALM 5:11

_____

_____

_____

_____

_____

_____

_____

PSALM 12:5

_____

_____

_____

_____

_____

_____

_____

_____

PSALM 20:1

_____
_____
_____
_____
_____
_____
_____
_____
_____

PSALM 59:1

_____
_____
_____
_____
_____
_____
_____
_____
_____

PSALM 17:8

_____
_____
_____
_____
_____
_____
_____
_____

PSALM 36:7

_____
_____
_____
_____
_____
_____
_____
_____
_____

PSALM 138:7

_____
_____
_____
_____
_____
_____
_____
_____

PSALM 121:5-6

_____
_____
_____
_____
_____
_____
_____
_____

PSALM 91:7-9

_____
_____
_____
_____
_____
_____
_____
_____
_____

PROVERBS 21:31

_____
_____
_____
_____
_____
_____
_____
_____
_____

Now, summarize below what you have learned through the passages. Look for a common theme.

_____

_____

_____

_____

_____

_____

_____

_____

_____

_____

_____

_____

_____

_____

_____

_____

_____

_____

_____

_____

_____

_____

_____

_____

_____

_____

_____

_____

_____

_____

_____

_____

REFLECTION TIME

When you feel like you are being attacked, what has been your response?

_____

_____

_____

_____

_____

_____

How do our scriptures in this chapter impact the way you handle adversity?

_____

_____

_____

_____

_____

_____

Which scripture passage speaks to you the most and why?

_____

_____

_____

_____

_____

_____

Write out a prayer thanking God for His protection, His comfort, and His shelter for you in the storms of life.

_____

_____

_____

_____

_____

_____

_____

Dear Jesus: Thank You that we can come to You when we are frightened or feel threatened for some reason. You are our Ultimate Protector, our Strong Tower against the enemy, and our Shelter in the storm. Please help us to stop looking for worldly solutions to what troubles us. Help us to know that all we need to do is to call out Your name, and You are there for us. Thank You! Amen.

CALL TO ACTION

In your journal, make a list of all the ways that you are feeling vulnerable, attacked, or fearful. Choose two or three of our scriptures and pray them over the list, asking God to cover you, protect you and strengthen you. Then make a "praise" list of how He is answering your prayers.

READY, SET, GO!

CHAPTER 9

HE IS OUR JOY IN TIMES OF TRIALS

"My brethren, count it all joy when you fall into various trials" (James 1:2)

DON'T YOU LOVE HOW DIRECT James is in his epistle? He doesn't sugarcoat anything or handhold his audience; he barely even says, "Hello." Instead, he cuts right to the chase with his message to his Jewish audience.

In all honesty, I find it difficult sometimes to find joy in the middle of a trial. I tend to whine about my circumstances. Woe is me. But as usual, God's Word gives us a different perspective that does not always please the flesh.

Let's define what James means when he tells us to count trials as joy. He does NOT mean that we have to take the attitude of, "Yippie, a trial!" I do not know anyone who wants them, looks forward to them, or misses them when life is on an even keel. What he is saying is that we should consider it joyful because of what it can produce in us. He went on to say that when we are in a trial, it can be a testing of our faith. And that testing will produce patience in us.

It is important to note that trials are not to be wasted. God has a perfect plan for all that He does and allows. It is a sad thing to go through hardship and not grow somehow from it. Even if the only thing we can say afterward is God is good and He is faithful. We may never know this side of heaven the purpose of the trial, but we can know with total certainty that God's loving hand is upon us. Growing closer to Jesus through the trial is its own reward.

There is a perfect example in the Bible of having joy through extreme trials. Take a look at this passage about Jesus:

"Looking unto Jesus, the Author and Finisher of our faith, who for the joy that was set before Him endured the cross, despising the shame, and has sat down at the right hand of the throne of God." (Hebrews 12:2) Jesus was about to face unbelievable physical suffering and separation from His Father, and He was going to bear the burden of taking all the punishment for our sins upon Himself. Yet He was able to feel joy because of the finished work of the cross and that He was returning to His Father and to His glory in heaven. Jesus also willingly gave His life for His sheep. He knew that His suffering was temporary and would have rewards beyond the pain He suffered.

"But rejoice to the extent that you partake of Christ's sufferings, that when His glory is revealed, you may also be glad with exceeding joy." (1 Peter 4:13) It is a glorious thing that we can partner with Jesus! When we were just sinners, we could not understand what the suffering of Christ meant and what the impact would be. Now as His children, we know that His glory will far outshine the sufferings and will even be a result of that suffering. As his children, we should be willing to partake in that for the glory which is coming soon.

"Whom having not seen you love. Though now you do not see Him, yet believing, you rejoice with joy inexpressible and full of glory." (1 Peter 1:8) I love this passage. Our earthly minds question how we can love someone or something we have never seen but have only read about. But this is where true faith comes in. To believe without seeing. Even now, with our limited minds, we as believers can rejoice in His goodness. I cannot even fathom what His full glory will be like when it is completely revealed!

Do you remember when Moses went up to Mt. Sinai? He had to be covered with a veil because the glory of God was too much for his earthly eyes. Even Paul, when he was taken up to the third heaven, couldn't even describe it. It was too much for him to take in. But one day, we will be face-to-face with Him. But with our heavenly eyes, we will be able to take in all His glory. And the sufferings we endured for His namesake will be worth every moment. No doubt, we will see that what we suffered here on earth did not come close to what we will see in Him.

"You will show me the path of life; in Your presence is fullness of joy; at Your right hand are pleasures forevermore." (Psalm 16:11) The path of life leads to a glorious relationship with Jesus. Can you imagine having nothing but pleasure and joy? That will be what heaven is like.

"*For the kingdom of God is not eating and drinking, but righteousness and peace and joy in the Holy Spirit."* (Romans 14:17) We need to remember that this life should not center around our physical or practical needs. You can have everything you want and still be empty. But living a life that is pleasing to God will give us so much more than that five-course meal, fancy car, or a bank account full of money. The temporal things will eventually fade away. But the peace and joy which comes from the Holy Spirit will always satisfy. Even when the temporal disappears. Let's study some scriptures about how we achieve this joy in the trials:

"Rejoice in the Lord always. Again I will say, rejoice!" (Philippians 4:4) So here we are instructed to rejoice always, even during the trials. There are some benefits to doing this. One, it keeps our eyes focused on Him, not on our circumstances. Another thing, our joyful attitude will make the trials easier to bear. How do we rejoice? We praise Him in song, word, and deed.

"A merry heart does good, like medicine, but a broken spirit dries the bones." (Proverbs 17:22) The condition of our heart does affect how we feel, act, and impact others. When we are joyful, we are lifted up. But a bad attitude drags us down and sucks the life out of everyone around us. That does not mean we put on a facade and pretend nothing is wrong. We are able to have joy and peace while in the trial.

"The hope of the righteous will be gladness, but the expectation of the wicked will perish." (Proverbs 10:28) When we have hope and peace in Jesus, we can experience joy in our hearts and souls. But the world will keep looking for hope in things that will never last. As the righteous can rest in the promise of eternal glory, the wicked will never be satisfied and has no true hope beyond the grave.

"And now my head shall be lifted up above my enemies all around me; therefore I will offer sacrifices of joy in His tabernacle; I will sing, yes, I will sing praises to the Lord." (Psalm 27:6) As I said before, there is nothing like a few praise songs to lift us out of the muck and mire of life. And as we experience true joy in Jesus, the enemy can have no power over us. Paul and Silas sang the shackles right off their hands while in prison!

"A man has joy by the answer of his mouth, and a word spoken in due season, how good it is!" (Proverbs 15:23) A word rightly spoken can lift someone out of their despair and truly bless them. But we need to be careful and be sure that this is coming from the Lord. We need to use discernment. Sometimes our well-meaning words of comfort can be more hurtful than helpful. Do you remember Job's friends? When they decided to start sharing their "wisdom" it backfired. "Miserable comforters are you all" was his response.

"For His anger is but for a moment, His favor is for life; weeping may endure for a night, but joy comes in the morning." (Psalm 30:5) This is a good reminder that God may be angry at us when we sin and must dole out some good old fashioned spankings now and then. But when this happens, we need to also remember that He chastens whom He loves (Hebrews 12:6). He is a forgiving God, so nothing can separate us from His love. He won't give up on us when we mess up. Like a loving father, He will pick us up, dust us off and kiss us on the cheek!

"You have turned for me my mourning into dancing; You have put off my sackcloth and clothed me with gladness." (Psalm 30:11) Jesus is always there waiting to comfort and strengthen us. He knows better than anyone the fruits of suffering. He is the ultimate Comforter. May we grow to be more like Him through the difficulties of this life.

"In the multitude of my anxieties within me, Your comforts delight my soul." (Psalm 94:19)

BIBLE STUDY AND JOURNAL TIME

Grab your bible, and dig into the chapter's scriptures! Don't forget to read the entire chapter to get the context. And record what the Lord has revealed to you in each passage. Pray for revelation before you begin.

JAMES 1:2 ("Anchor" passage)

_____
_____
_____
_____
_____
_____
_____
_____

HEBREWS 12:2

_____
_____
_____
_____
_____
_____
_____

1 PETER 4:13

_____
_____
_____
_____
_____
_____
_____

1 PETER 1:8

_____
_____
_____
_____
_____
_____
_____
_____

PSALM 16:11

_____
_____
_____
_____
_____
_____
_____
_____

ROMANS 14:17

_____
_____
_____
_____
_____
_____
_____
_____

PHILIPPIANS 4:4

_____
_____
_____
_____
_____
_____
_____
_____
_____

PROVERBS 17:22

_____
_____
_____
_____
_____
_____
_____
_____

PROVERBS 10:28

_____
_____
_____
_____
_____
_____
_____
_____

PSALM 27:6

_____
_____
_____
_____
_____
_____
_____
_____
_____
_____

PROVERBS 15:23

_____
_____
_____
_____
_____
_____
_____
_____

PSALM 30:5

_____
_____
_____
_____
_____
_____
_____
_____

PSALM 30:11

_____
_____
_____
_____
_____
_____
_____
_____
_____

PSALM 94:19

_____
_____
_____
_____
_____
_____
_____
_____
_____

Now, summarize below what you have learned through the passages. Look for a common theme.

_____
_____
_____
_____
_____
_____
_____
_____
_____
_____
_____
_____
_____
_____
_____
_____
_____
_____
_____
_____
_____
_____
_____
_____
_____
_____
_____
_____
_____
_____
_____
_____

REFLECTION TIME

What is your reaction to the thought of counting trials as joy?

_____

_____

_____

_____

_____

_____

How would being joyful impact your response during a trial?

_____

_____

_____

_____

_____

_____

How do you find strength knowing that you are partnering with Jesus in trials?

_____

_____

_____

_____

_____

_____

Write out a prayer thanking God for the joy to be found in trials and for the strength to overcome them.

_____

_____

_____

_____

_____

Dear Jesus: it is hard to wrap our earthly minds around the thought of being joyful in our trials. But we know that You are asking us to look beyond our circumstances and trust that You are working in them. When we get down or worried, please, through the Holy Spirit, remind us of what You suffered for us. Thank you. In Your Name, amen!

CALL TO ACTION

In your journal, write about a particularly difficult trial that you have experienced. Explore your attitude then, and how these passages you have studied might have had an impact on how you handled it.

READY, SET, GO!

CHAPTER 10

HE IS OUR VICTORY IN THE BATTLE

"There is therefore now no condemnation to those who are in Christ Jesus, who do not walk according to the flesh, but according to the Spirit." (Romans 8:1)

THERE IS A NEVER-ENDING BATTLE between our flesh and our spirit. Deep down, I think we know what is good or bad for us and what is right or wrong. Oh, but the temptations that Satan taunts us with! I remember, quite a while ago, I was going to give up caffeine for 30 days. My resolve was strong. Well, for at least the first 30 minutes of my self-imposed fast. The strange thing was I have never been a huge coffee drinker, maybe a cup in the morning. But you'd think I had been on a caffeine drip the way I was craving it. Oh no, now I want a soda! Sadly, it was only 10:00 in the morning. We always seem to want what we can't have, don't we? That is the way of human nature, I guess. Satan was bugging me big time.

I was faithful to my commitment. Only because I made a "covenant" with God that I was going to give up this evil stuff. I felt that if I gave into the temptation, I would let God down. The last few days, I was in countdown mode. I couldn't wait to pour that steaming, freshly brewed cup of Joe. But do you know what? It was terrible! I was so disappointed. I had built it up in my mind, only to be let down by reality.

Sin is like that. The enemy waves a big shiny object in front of us, trying to persuade us that we need whatever it is. It will satisfy our deepest longing, give us immense pleasure, and fill our needs. We buy his lie hook, line, and sinker. Then after he reels us in and we give into our flesh, he pulls the shame card out-the Condemnation trap. "Loser!" " How could you do that?" "God can't possibly love a sinner like you." We believe the lie, hide from God, and beat ourselves up. (Does this remind you of the antics of Satan in the Garden of Eden?) Sometimes we may even think, well, what's the point? I can't do this. Score one for Satan.

But take a good look at our anchor verse. There is no condemnation when we are children of God. And please understand that temptations come from the enemy, not from God. So does condemnation. God will correct and convict but not condemn us for our actions or thoughts.

"For sin shall not have dominion over you, for you are not under law but under grace." (Romans 6:14) We can't be victorious in overcoming our sinful nature apart from Jesus. But when Jesus abolished the law and brought the new covenant of grace, we were given freedom from sin and bondage.

"But thanks be to God, who gives us the victory through our Lord Jesus Christ." (1 Corinthians 15:57) As followers of Jesus, we have the Holy Spirit living inside us. Through the death and resurrection of Jesus, we have been set free from the bondage of sin.

"Yet in all these things we are more than conquerors through Him who loved us." (Romans 8:37) Oh, there will be battles along the way. But we are victorious in Christ and more than conquerors before the battle even begins.

Unfortunately, there are more battles than the one with our flesh. The world does not like us. No surprise there. Jesus himself said this would be so. Anything different that doesn't fit its agenda is automatically an enemy. But…

"For whatever is born of God overcomes the world. And this is the victory that has overcome the world-our faith." (1 John 5:4) Our faith has helped us to overcome the world. We have to live *in* it; there is no way around that. But we are not to be *of* the world. That is, to be partakers of

sinful, Godless ideals and behaviors. As Christians, we are to be set apart from that and live the life that Jesus calls us to.

"These things I have spoken to you, that in Me you may have peace. In the world you will have tribulation; but be of good cheer, I have overcome the world." (John 16:33) Sometimes I can get so discouraged and upset with the rampant evil that surrounds us every day. But I need to remember that all of this is temporary, that Jesus has overcome the devil, and one day He will make everything right again. If I allow the darkness to overwhelm me, I become neutralized in this battle. And make no mistake about it; we are in a constant spiritual battle.

"What then shall we say to these things? If God is for us, who can be against us?" (Romans 8:31) Isn't it reassuring to know that God is on our side? We have a powerful adversary in Satan, but he is no match for God!

"And the Lord said to Joshua, 'Do not fear them, for I have delivered them into your hand; not a man of them shall stand before you.'" (Joshua 10:8) Joshua was a mighty warrior. He fought many battles in the name of the Lord. He knew that God was on his side.

"O Death, where is your sting? O Hades, where is your victory?" (1 Corinthians 15:55) Death and hell have no power over the believer. Our fleshly body will die, but our spirit will live on with Jesus.

"Through God, we will do valiantly, for it is He who shall tread down our enemies." (Psalm 108:13) We don't have to fight our adversary. God is the True Victor. Don't for a second think that David took down Goliath simply through the strength of a few rocks. It was the power of God behind him.

"But you are a chosen generation, a royal priesthood, a holy nation, His own special people, that you may proclaim the praises of Him who called you out of darkness into His marvelous light." (1 Peter 2:9) I love being one of God's kids. We were pulled out of the miry clay and set upon the rock of Jesus!

"So when this corruptible has put on incorruption, and this mortal has put on immortality, then shall be brought to pass the saying that

is written: 'Death is swallowed up in victory.'" (1 Corinthians 15:54) Even though our fleshly bodies will one day perish, we will live on in incorruptibility as we are called up to heaven. We will never be more alive than in that moment!

"These will make war with the Lamb, and the Lamb will overcome them, for He is Lord of lords and King of kings; and those who are with Him are called, chosen, and faithful." (Revelation 17:14) What a glorious day that will be when Jesus will set everything right, take His rightful place as King of kings and Lord of lords! Satan and all his evil cohorts will be put away forever. And those of us who are God's children will be with Him when He establishes His kingdom. The ultimate victory!

So, our victory comes from Jesus. Stop trying to do things in your own strength. Whether it be fighting addiction, saving your marriage, raising prodigal kids, or just trying to navigate this crazy thing called life. We have Jesus on our side. Satan can't touch us as believers if God says no. Oh, he will try his dead level best to derail us, separate us from God, even if it is in the moment. But if we keep our eyes on the prize, striving toward the upward call of God in Christ Jesus, we will lead a victorious life. Whenever you feel like you are drowning and can't see a way out, look up to the Author and Finisher of your faith, Jesus Christ. He will lead you to victory every single time!

"Now thanks be to God who always leads us in triumph in Christ, and through us diffuses the fragrance of His knowledge in every place." (2 Corinthians 2:14)

BIBLE STUDY AND JOURNAL TIME

Grab your bible, and dig into the chapter's scriptures! Don't forget to read the entire chapter to get the context. And record what the Lord has revealed to you in each passage. Pray for revelation before you begin.

ROMANS 8:1 ("Anchor" passage)

_____

_____

_____

_____

_____

_____

_____

_____

ROMANS 6:14

_____

_____

_____

_____

_____

_____

1 CORINTHIANS 15:57

_____

_____

_____

_____

_____

_____

ROMANS 8:37

_____

_____

_____

_____

_____

_____

_____

_____

_____

1 JOHN 5:4

_____

_____

_____

_____

_____

_____

_____

_____

JOHN 16:33

_____

_____

_____

_____

_____

_____

_____

_____

ROMANS 8:31

_____
_____
_____
_____
_____
_____
_____
_____
_____

JOSHUA 10:8

_____
_____
_____
_____
_____
_____
_____
_____
_____

1 CORINTHIANS 15:55

_____
_____
_____
_____
_____
_____
_____
_____
_____

PSALM 108:13

_____

_____

_____

_____

_____

_____

_____

_____

1 PETER 2:9

_____

_____

_____

_____

_____

_____

_____

1 CORINTHIANS 15:54

_____

_____

_____

_____

_____

_____

_____

REVELATION 17:14

_____

_____

_____

_____

_____

_____

_____

_____

_____

2 CORINTHIANS 2:14

_____

_____

_____

_____

_____

_____

_____

_____

_____

Now, summarize below what you have learned through the passages. Look for a common theme.

_____
_____
_____
_____
_____
_____
_____
_____
_____
_____
_____
_____
_____
_____
_____
_____
_____
_____
_____
_____
_____
_____
_____
_____
_____
_____

REFLECTION TIME

Describe a time when you tried to have victory in your own strength.

_____

_____

_____

_____

_____

What would have changed if you had given the battle to Jesus?

_____

_____

_____

_____

_____

How does knowing that you are victorious in Jesus give you peace?

_____

_____

_____

_____

_____

Write out a prayer thanking God that He goes before you in all things.

_____

_____

_____

_____

_____

Dear Heavenly Father: Sometimes we feel overwhelmed and defeated in our lives. But we thank You that through Your Son we can claim victory over the enemy, death and sin. Help us to rely on You for our strength and courage, just as David and Joshua did. We are mighty in You, Lord. Thank You. Amen!

CALL TO ACTION

In your journal, write about some of the victories you have achieved through Jesus. Then list some that you tried to fight on your own. Compare and contrast the two "strategies".

READY, SET, GO!

CHAPTER 11

HE IS OUR MERCY WHEN WE STUMBLE

"Have mercy upon me, O God, according to Your lovingkindness; according to the multitude of Your tender mercies. Blot out my transgressions. Wash me thoroughly from my iniquity, and cleanse me from my sin." (Psalm 51:1-2)

WE ARE A GENERATION OBSESSED with our bodies and how they appear. We spend hours and tons of money to impress other people who are so busy doing the same thing they don't notice us. Check this out- Mary Jo spends an hour in the morning making herself look and smell good, only to hop in the car and light up a cigarette. She ends up reeking of the smoke, and her hair and clothes smell awful Yuck! She pops a breath mint in her mouth and sprays herself with perfume, hoping to cover up the stench. It's all a mask; it doesn't wash her clean. She still carries it with her. Unrepentant sin is a lot like that. But the main stench is coming from the heart. It needs to be dealt with rather than covered up.

I would have had a rough time in the Old Testament days. The thought of having to offer blood sacrifices for the atonement of my sins makes me squeamish. The laws were stringent, and there were 613 of them. I fear I would have been in perpetual "time out". I would virtually squeak from all the ceremonial cleansing! Until I messed up again.

Thankfully, when Jesus came to this earth, His mission was to abolish the laws of the old covenant and provide us with the law of grace. No longer were the bloody sacrifices of animals required for atonement. Jesus became the atonement. His blood was shed to cover our sins and to wash us clean. He took our place and bore our sins.

Another wonderful thing happened. When Jesus died on the cross, the temple veil was torn in two. The barricade between God and us was removed. We no longer need priests to intercede for us. We can come boldly to the throne of grace. We have a direct line, if you will, to the Holy of Holies.

The biblical definition of mercy is God bestowing kindness and compassion on us. Instead of giving us the punishment we deserve, God withholds His judgment on us. It's something He gives us every single day. If I were punished for every wrong attitude, behavior, or thought that displeased God, I would be in more trouble than the Israelites were! But His mercy and grace are new every morning. What a wonderful Savior, isn't He? Check this verse out:

"Through the Lord's mercies we are not consumed, because His compassions fail not." (Lamentations 3:22) If it weren't for His unending mercy, I would be utterly destroyed by my sin.

"Be merciful to me, O Lord, for I cry to You all day long. Rejoice the soul of Your servant, for to You, O Lord, I lift up my soul. For You, Lord, are good, and ready to forgive, and abundant in mercy to all those who call upon You." (Psalm 86:3-5) Psalm 86 was a prayer of David's. He understood our human need for constant mercy. Sometimes that need is moment to moment. But he also understood our need to seek the Lord and cry out for His mercy.

"The Lord is longsuffering and abundant in mercy, forgiving iniquity and transgression; but He by no means clears the guilty, visiting the iniquity of the fathers on the children to the third and fourth generation." (Numbers 14:18) We must understand that God's mercy and forgiveness are not a license to sin. You may have heard the expression, "Ask for permission now or for forgiveness later." The world may think like that, but it shouldn't be the mindset of a child of God

"For judgment is without mercy to the one who has shown no mercy. Mercy triumphs over judgment." (James 2:13) How many times have we asked judgment on those around us but sought mercy on us when we do the same thing?

"Blessed are the merciful, for they shall obtain mercy" (Matthew 5:7) A good rule of thumb is if you want to get, you've got to give! But check the motive of your heart. We want to have a merciful heart because of Christ living in us. It shouldn't be motivated by what we get out of it.

"He who covers his sins will not prosper, but whoever confesses and forsakes them will have mercy." (Proverbs 28:13) There is no hiding from God. Remember in the garden? God saw all that Adam and Eve had done. They sinned big time and tried to hide it by covering their nakedness with fig leaves. They didn't fool God, though. He knew their actions and, most importantly, their hearts. But in His mercy, He covered their sins with animal skins, the first blood sacrifice. And although He showed them mercy, there were consequences for their sin. And all of mankind has felt it.

"Surely goodness and mercy shall follow me all the days of my life, and I shall dwell in the house of the Lord forever." (Psalm 23:6) It is a lovely reality to know that in this life, as His child, I am covered by His goodness and mercy. And then to be able to abide in His house when He calls me home? It can't get any better than that!

"For He says to Moses, 'I will have mercy on whom I have mercy, and I will have compassion on whom I have compassion.'" (Romans 9:15) God is an infinite source of mercy and compassion. But He chooses when and to whom He will dispense it.

However, for this reason, I obtained mercy, that in me first Jesus Christ might show all longsuffering, as a pattern to those who are going to believe on Him for everlasting life." (1 Timothy 1:16) I am so glad that God is infinitely patient, loving, and merciful with this wretched sinner!

"Therefore the Lord will wait, that He may be gracious to you; and therefore He will be exalted, that He may have mercy on you. For the Lord is a God of justice; blessed are all those who wait for Him." (Isaiah 30:18) God is a God of infinite patience through our obstinance, rebellion, and even idolatry. But His mercy is there for us when we turn from our wicked ways and wait on Him. He was far more patient

127

than I would have been with the Israelites. Honestly, I can relate more to the Israelites than I care to admit!

"But go and learn what this means: 'I desire mercy and not sacrifice.' For I did not come to call the righteous, but sinners to repentance." (Matthew 9:13) The Pharisees were giving Jesus a hard time about associating with tax collectors because they were considered the lowest of the low. But He set them straight about His mission. He came to seek and save the lost, not the righteous. Mercy was what was called for, not a ritualistic sacrifice. And Jesus extended the ultimate mercy when He died on the cross.

So there you have it. Mercy, God's never-ending grace, and compassion are on us. They are new every morning, as the song goes. He loves us so much that He is eager to lavish them on us. But we need to do our part. We need to cry out for them and then receive them. Our hearts need to be repentant.

I am so thankful that Jesus chose to become the sacrificial Lamb to atone for our sins. If He didn't, we would die in them. Instead, we are free from the guilt and shame that comes upon us when we sin and repent. Mercy is one way that God shows His glory. This doesn't give us free rein to sin and then take for granted that God will forgive us. Remember, He always looks to the heart. But we can come directly to the throne of grace and feel His loving arms of grace, compassion, and forgiveness.

"But You, O Lord, are a God full of compassion, and gracious, longsuffering and abundant in mercy and truth." (Psalm 86:15) I, for one, couldn't be more thankful!

"Let us therefore come boldly to the throne of grace, that we may obtain mercy and find grace to help in time of need." (Hebrews 4:16)

BIBLE STUDY AND JOURNAL TIME

Grab your bible, and dig into the chapter's scriptures! Don't forget to read the entire chapter to get the context. And record what the Lord has revealed to you in each passage. Pray for revelation before you begin.

PSALM 51:1-2 ("Anchor" passage)

_____

_____

_____

_____

_____

_____

_____

_____

LAMENTATIONS 3:22

_____

_____

_____

_____

_____

_____

_____

PSALM 86:3-5

_____

_____

_____

_____

_____

_____

_____

NUMBERS 14:18

_____
_____
_____
_____
_____
_____
_____
_____
_____

JAMES 2:13

_____
_____
_____
_____
_____
_____
_____
_____

MATTHEW 5:7

_____
_____
_____
_____
_____
_____
_____
_____

PROVERBS 28:13

_____
_____
_____
_____
_____
_____
_____
_____
_____
_____

PSALM 23:6

_____
_____
_____
_____
_____
_____
_____
_____

ROMANS 9:15

_____
_____
_____
_____
_____
_____
_____
_____

1 TIMOTHY 1:16

ISAIAH 30:18

MATTHEW 9:13

PSALM 86:15

_____

_____

_____

_____

_____

_____

_____

_____

HEBREWS 4:16

_____

_____

_____

_____

_____

_____

_____

_____

Now, summarize below what you have learned through the passages. Look for a common theme.

_____

_____

_____

_____

_____

_____

_____

_____

_____

_____

_____

_____

_____

_____

_____

_____

_____

_____

_____

_____

_____

_____

_____

_____

_____

_____

_____

_____

_____

_____

_____

_____

REFLECTION TIME

Has there been a situation in your life where you were shown mercy that you really didn't deserve?

_____

_____

_____

_____

_____

_____

How about a time when you weren't? How did you handle the "injustice"?

_____

_____

_____

_____

_____

_____

How does God's grace and mercy impact your walk as a believer?

_____

_____

_____

_____

_____

_____

Write out a prayer thanking God for His mercy and grace.

_____

_____

_____

_____

_____

_____

Dear Heavenly Father: We are so grateful for Your never-ending grace and mercy. We don't deserve it. You have every right to cast judgment on us for all of our wicked deeds, yet Your infinite love for us spares us from the harshness we deserve. I pray we strive to be as forgiving and merciful to others as You are to us each and every day. Thank you, Jesus! Amen

CALL TO ACTION

Truth time! Think about situations where you wanted for mercy for yourself, but thought justice was called for in someone else in that same scenario. Be honest with yourself. How can we have more compassion on others when they wrong or hurt us? Journal your thoughts.

READY, SET, GO!

CHAPTER 12

HE IS OUR FREEDOM FROM BONDAGE

"Therefore if the Son makes you free, you shall be free indeed." (John 8:36)

FREEDOM IS A PRECIOUS THING. Hundreds of thousands of military personnel have paid the ultimate price throughout America's history. Because of these sacrifices, we have the freedom to live the kind of life we want. Our constitution gives us certain inalienable rights. The term, "Don't tread on me" goes back to 1775, when we sought independence from British rule. Our nation was torn in two almost a century later over primarily the issue of slavery. More than 600,000 men perished, and families were torn apart. Brother fought against brother. It was a tragic time in our nation's history. Not only military folk, but police officers face that real possibility every time they put on their uniform. Innocent bloodshed is the highest price paid for freedom. To be willing to lay one's life down for others is truly courageous. Many men and women have paid the price for freedom.

Our Lord and Savior, Jesus, did exactly that. It was through the shedding of His innocent blood that we can have the ultimate freedom. Free from the guilt and burden of sin. He willingly went to the cross, endured the shame, took all our sins upon Him, and became the blood sacrifice that God requires for the atonement of sin. We became washed clean.

As you study the Bible, you will find many paradoxes. Statements or ideas that appear contradictory to us. Here we have some prime examples: *"For he who is called in the Lord while a slave is the Lord's freedman. Likewise he who is called while free is Christ's slave."* (1 Corinthians 7:22)

"And having been set free from sin, you became slaves of righteousness." (Romans 6:18)

I can hear you asking, "How can we be free if we give up sin and then become slaves? Isn't it just exchanging one entrapment for another?" That is an excellent question. But we have to look deeper into the issue. Once again, we need to stop looking at God's Word through the lens of the world. We have to determine first what we are being freed from. We have been in bondage to sin from the day we were born. Sin entered the world through the fall in the Garden of Eden. We have been prisoners of it ever since. Before Jesus came, atonement for sin came through animal sacrifices. But when Jesus went to the cross, He became the substitute for that, and once for all made atonement for us. No longer do we have to pay the penalty of sin. Eternally speaking, that is. I am not talking about not having to go to jail when you commit a crime. There are still consequences for bad behavior.

Jesus has given us new life spiritually and saved us from eternal damnation. Because of this, we are slaves to Christ. But again, not as the world sees slavery. There is no degradation or hardship. Freedom in Christ gives us peace and joy. We can't repay Jesus for what He did for us. We have been purchased by God. But it is such an awesome thing. If there are feelings of oppression or bondage of being a Christian, I contend those come from not truly understanding what it means to follow Christ. Man has put rules and regulations on just about everything. The ten commandments eventually became 613 laws because legalistic Pharisees felt the people had to follow everything meticulously. Then Jesus came along and blew that theory right out of the water. Not only did He abolish the 613, but He narrowed the whole thing down to two commands. Love God and love others. See what happens when men get in there? They muddy things up and create a huge mess. God's way is so much simpler!

"But now having been set free from sin, and having become slaves of God, you have your fruit to holiness, and the end, everlasting life." (Romans 6:22) When Jesus came to save man, He freed us from all that garbage I spoke of before. Hallelujah!

"What then? Shall we sin because we are not under law but under grace? Certainly not!" (Romans 6:15) Freedom in Christ doesn't mean that we have the right to do whatever we want regardless, but it means we have the ability, through Him, to do what is right. We are free from the desire to lead a sinful life. We will want to lead a life that is pleasing to Him. The world puts shackles on us in so many ways. Isn't it wonderful to be free from that? When I see a person give their life over to Jesus, I picture the chains of sin and shame falling off them. You can almost see them start to breathe again. Tears of joy wash away the years of sadness.

"And you shall know the truth, and the truth shall make you free." (John 8:32) There is nothing so entangling as a lie. Its purpose is to deceive, distort, manipulate, and control others. Satan has been using this trick since the beginning of time. But while Satan cannot tell the truth, Jesus IS Truth. And truth is liberating, even if we may not always like it.

"For this is the will of God, that by doing good you may put to silence the ignorance of foolish men— as free, yet not using liberty as a cloak for vice, but as bondservants of God." (1 Peter 2:15-16) We have been given many liberties as children of God. But we have to use them responsibly. Some people take the attitude that they are free to sin because God will forgive them if they ask. I'd be careful going down that road. To me, it is a form of mocking God and all that He is.

"All things are lawful for me, but all things are not helpful. All things are lawful for me, but I will not be brought under the power of any." (1 Corinthians 6:12) Paul is warning us that just because we *can* do something, that doesn't mean that we *should* do it. Anything that takes the place of Jesus in our hearts or lives, which might cause a brother or a sister to stumble, or that might become too important to us, we should probably avoid it. There is nothing wrong, per se, with eating a fast food meal. But if it becomes a problem for you while you are trying to lose weight, if it becomes the rule rather than the exception in your diet, if having one (like that first potato chip) will derail you, then that can easily become a stumbling block for your health quest. Some people can have a glass of wine, while others need to abstain. The best rule of thumb is to ask yourself if what you are about to do or engage in helps or hinders your walk with Jesus, or be a bad example for someone not strong in their walk.

"For you, brethren, have been called to liberty; only do not use liberty as an opportunity for the flesh, but through love serve one another." (Galatians 5:13) Again, avoid the mentality that you can do anything you want. We must always be seeking to please God and be a blessing to others around us.

"Stand fast therefore in the liberty by which Christ has made us free, and do not be entangled again with a yoke of bondage." (Galatians 5:1) There are many religions that, with all their rites and rituals, can cause us to feel like we are in bondage. And so many of them are not biblically based. There is no place in a relationship with Jesus for legalism. The harshest words Jesus had were for the legalists of His day.

"And I will walk at liberty, for I seek Your precepts." (Psalm 119:45) Following the teachings of the Bible frees us up. And as stated before, with the power of the Holy Spirit in us, we should desire to do what He calls us to do. It should not be a burden.

"Therefore let it be known to you, brethren, that through this Man is preached to you the forgiveness of sins and by Him everyone who believes is justified from all things from which you could not be justified by the law of Moses." (Acts 13:38-39) The law of Moses could not justify, only condemn. Through Jesus we are forgiven and declared holy.

"For the law of the Spirit of life in Christ Jesus has made me free from the law of sin and death." (Romans 8:2) Because we are in Christ Jesus, we are free from the curse of sin and death. He has made us free! We are no longer slaves to sin. He has rescued us from eternal hell and damnation. He deserves all that we can give Him. To love Him with all our heart, souls, and minds and to love others as He has loved us.

"Now the Lord is the Spirit; and where the Spirit of the Lord is, there is liberty." (2 Corinthians 3:17)

BIBLE STUDY AND JOURNAL TIME

Grab your bible, and dig into the chapter's scriptures! Don't forget to read the entire chapter to get the context. And record what the Lord has revealed to you in each passage. Pray for revelation before you begin.

JOHN 8:36 ("Anchor" passage)

_____

_____

_____

_____

_____

_____

_____

_____

1 CORINTHIANS 7:22

_____

_____

_____

_____

_____

_____

_____

ROMANS 6:18

_____

_____

_____

_____

_____

_____

_____

ROMANS 6:22

_____
_____
_____
_____
_____
_____
_____
_____

ROMANS 6:15

_____
_____
_____
_____
_____
_____
_____
_____

JOHN 8:32

_____
_____
_____
_____
_____
_____
_____
_____

1 PETER 2:15-16

_____
_____
_____
_____
_____
_____
_____
_____
_____

1 CORINTHIANS 6:12

_____
_____
_____
_____
_____
_____
_____
_____
_____

GALATIANS 5:13

_____
_____
_____
_____
_____
_____
_____
_____
_____

GALATIANS 5:1

_____
_____
_____
_____
_____
_____
_____
_____
_____

PSALM 119:45

_____
_____
_____
_____
_____
_____
_____
_____
_____

ACTS 13:38-39

_____
_____
_____
_____
_____
_____
_____
_____
_____

ROMANS 8:2

_____

_____

_____

_____

_____

_____

_____

_____

2 CORINTHIANS 3:17

_____

_____

_____

_____

_____

_____

_____

_____

_____

Now, summarize below what you have learned through the passages. Look for a common theme.

_____
_____
_____
_____
_____
_____
_____
_____
_____
_____
_____
_____
_____
_____
_____
_____
_____
_____
_____
_____
_____
_____
_____
_____
_____
_____
_____
_____
_____
_____
_____

REFLECTION TIME

Contrast or compare the difference between freedom in the world and freedom in Christ.

_____

_____

_____

_____

_____

_____

How could our liberties in Jesus cause others to stumble?

_____

_____

_____

_____

_____

_____

Describe a time when that may have happened, or when you stumbled.

_____

_____

_____

_____

_____

_____

Write out a prayer thanking God for the freedom we gain from His sacrifice.

_____

_____

_____

_____

_____

_____

Dear Heavenly Father:

It is so awesome and humbling to know that Your sufferings on the cross gave us freedom from sin. We don't deserve it, and if we gave You everything we have, it could never come close to repaying You. Thank You that You are not asking for that payment; it was a free gift. And we are eternally grateful! In Your Name, Amen!

CALL TO ACTION

Self-evaluation time. Take a hard look into your heart and see what God may be asking you to give up in order to have freedom and victory in that area. Write it in your journal, and ask Him to give you the strength to do so.

READY, SET, GO!

CHAPTER 13

HE IS OUR SALVATION WHEN WE ARE LOST

"For God so loved the world that He gave His only begotten Son, that whoever believes in Him should not perish but have everlasting life. For God did not send His Son into the world to condemn the world, but that the world through Him might be saved." (John 3:16-17)

OUR ANCHOR VERSE FOR THIS chapter is arguably one of the most quoted passages in the Bible. Can you imagine someone loving you so much that they would sacrifice their child for you? I can't fathom it. I could see a parent making the sacrifice for his or her child, but not sacrificing the child for someone who is steeped in sin and filth, which we are. Paul says our righteousness is like filthy rags.

"For scarcely for a righteous man will one die; yet perhaps for a good man someone would even dare to die. But God demonstrates His own love toward us, in that while we were still sinners, Christ died for us." (Romans 5:7-8) Yet our loving Father, the Creator of heaven and earth and everything in it, decided we were worth the price. It doesn't matter what sin you have committed or how "good" you are. We are all equal at the foot of the cross. So why would He make such a sacrifice?

"He has delivered us from the power of darkness and conveyed us into the kingdom of the Son of His love, in whom we have redemption through His blood, the forgiveness of sins." (Colossians 1:13-14) There is no way I could fulfill the requirement for forgiveness and eternal life. God's standard is too high. He has always required a blood sacrifice. So in His mercy, He provided that sacrifice through the shedding

of His Son's blood. Every sin committed by every human being that has walked the face of this earth, or will walk it, was put upon Jesus on the cross. We have been forgiven and washed clean.

"But He was wounded for our transgressions, He was bruised for our iniquities; the chastisement for our peace was upon Him, and by His stripes, we are healed." (Isaiah 53:5) The question begs, especially by the skeptic, WHY does God love me so much that He would make this sacrifice? Many reasons come to mind, but you need to understand God's nature. Not only *does* He love, but He *is* love. It is His very nature. So, He lavishes that love on us. We were created in His image, which is love. That love is unconditional as well. He is not fickle like humans, who are ruled by emotions, swaying with every passing wind. His love is steadfast. Even after being brutalized on the cross, cursed at and mocked, Jesus looked up to His Father and asked forgiveness for us. I don't see many humans being so forgiving and for far lesser offenses.

Through the years, there have been many false teachings and concepts about forgiveness and how we can go to heaven. Some think if our good deeds outweigh our bad ones, then the scale is in our favor and we are in. Others believe that everyone gets a free pass. Another teaching is that you must earn your way to heaven through good works. Or, after you die, a loved one can pray for your salvation. All roads lead to heaven. Love is enough, they say. Let me tell you, none of that is correct. Jesus tells us Himself:

"Jesus said to him, 'I am the way, the truth, and the life. No one comes to the Father except through Me.'" (John 14:6) Jesus is the true Living God. There is none like Him. He is not *a* way; He is the *only* way. He conquered sin and death when He died and rose again. Jesus is the one true Mediator between God and us. We don't have to go through a priest; we have direct access to the Father!

"Nor is there salvation in any other, for there is no other name under heaven given among men by which we must be saved." (Acts 4:12) Outside of Jesus, every other god is a false god. They have no power to save. Look at every religious leader that ever existed. When they died, they stayed dead. Jesus is alive! All the others were just mortal men. They were

not given the power to do anything for us. They can only lead us astray with false teachings. Jesus is not only alive, but He is alive forevermore! He is seated at the right hand of the Father, living to make intercession for us. He alone has the power to save. But what about this works thing? Don't I have to do good deeds to earn my way into heaven? As the apostle Paul would say, "Certainly not!" Here is what he does say about it:

"For by grace you have been saved through faith, and that not of yourselves; it is the gift of God, not of works, lest anyone should boast." (Ephesians 2:8-9) There is nothing we can do to earn it. It is a gift, ours for the taking. This may be hard to believe, and we may be skeptical. Too easy, you might say. Okay, then study this passage and do these things:

"That if you confess with your mouth the Lord Jesus and believe in your heart that God has raised Him from the dead, you will be saved. For with the heart, one believes unto righteousness, and with the mouth, confession is made unto salvation." (Romans 10:9-10) We do need to ask for forgiveness for our sins. But if your heart is sincere, it's a done deal. God made it easy for us. Jesus did all the heavy lifting. Why does man always want to complicate things? (Remember when we studied about the ten commandments turning into 613…) And then a beautiful thing happens:

"Therefore, if anyone is in Christ, he is a new creation; old things have passed away; behold, all things have become new." (2 Corinthians 5:17) As soon as we confess and receive, we are washed clean from our sins, and we become a new creature in Christ. All the old, dirty things that have been burdening us are swept away. We have a new lease on life. Eternal life! A common question our skeptic friend might throw at us is what about that person in the Mongolian desert who hasn't heard about Jesus? God has that covered too!

"Therefore He is also able to save to the uttermost those who come to God through Him since He always lives to make intercession for them." (Hebrews 7:25) God will meet a person where he is. He is a fair and just God. He won't hold someone accountable for what they don't know. But you would be surprised at how many ways you can find God. He is there in the sunrise, in the eyes of a newborn baby.

"For the Son of Man has come to seek and to save that which was lost." (Luke 19:10) Jesus didn't come to overthrow the Roman government like many people in His day thought. His kingdom will be established on this earth when He comes back. And we get to come with Him. What a glorious day that will be!

It seems like every Christian has a friend or a loved one who doesn't want to surrender. You may have been praying for years for them. You may be losing heart, and we may be getting impatient as we wait for His return. But God knows the heart of every man. He is infinitely patient. He knows what it will take to open their eyes. Keep praying!

"The Lord is not slack concerning His promise, as some count slackness, but is longsuffering toward us, not willing that any should perish but that all should come to repentance." (2 Peter 3:9) I'm so thankful that He didn't decide to come for His church before I made the decision to follow Him all those years ago!

"For He says: 'In an acceptable time I have heard you, and in the day of salvation I have helped you.' Behold, now is the accepted time; behold, now is the day of salvation." (2 Corinthians 6:2) He is calling us to Him. Today is the day. We need to heed His voice. Although He doesn't want anyone to perish, there will be a day, and I believe it is in the not-too-distant future when He will come for His bride. Those who don't accept Him will be left behind. The cost is high for those who reject Him. But for those who receive Jesus as their Lord and Savior, there will be peace and joy forevermore!

"For the wages of sin is death, but the gift of God is eternal life in Christ Jesus our Lord." (Romans 6:23)

BIBLE STUDY AND JOURNAL TIME

Grab your bible, and dig into the chapter's scriptures! Don't forget to read the entire chapter to get the context. And record what the Lord has revealed to you in each passage. Pray for revelation before you begin.

JOHN 3:16-17 ("Anchor" passage)

_____
_____
_____
_____
_____
_____
_____
_____

ROMANS 5:7-8

_____
_____
_____
_____
_____
_____
_____
_____

COLOSSIANS 1:13-14

_____
_____
_____
_____
_____
_____
_____

ISAIAH 53:5

JOHN 14:6

ACTS 4:12

EPHESIANS 2:8-9

_____

_____

_____

_____

_____

_____

_____

_____

ROMANS 10:9-10

_____

_____

_____

_____

_____

_____

_____

_____

2 CORINTHIANS 5:17

_____

_____

_____

_____

_____

_____

_____

_____

HEBREWS 7:25

_____
_____
_____
_____
_____
_____
_____
_____
_____

LUKE 19:10

_____
_____
_____
_____
_____
_____
_____
_____

2 PETER 3:9

_____
_____
_____
_____
_____
_____
_____
_____
_____

2 CORINTHIANS 6:2

_____
_____
_____
_____
_____
_____
_____
_____
_____

ROMANS 6:23

_____
_____
_____
_____
_____
_____
_____
_____
_____

Now, summarize below what you have learned through the passages. Look for a common theme.

_____

_____

_____

_____

_____

_____

_____

_____

_____

_____

_____

_____

_____

_____

_____

_____

_____

_____

_____

_____

_____

_____

_____

_____

_____

_____

_____

_____

_____

_____

_____

_____

REFLECTION TIME

Think about when you became a Christian. Describe your feelings then.

_____

_____

_____

_____

_____

_____

How was the gospel shared with you?

_____

_____

_____

_____

_____

How do you feel about sharing the gospel to unbelievers?

_____

_____

_____

_____

_____

Write out a prayer thanking God for the free gift of salvation.

_____

_____

_____

_____

_____

_____

Dear Heavenly Father:

It is so awesome and humbling to know that Your sufferings on the cross gave us freedom from sin. We don't deserve it, and if we gave You everything we have, it could never come close to repaying YOU. Thank You that You are not asking for that payment; it was a free gift. And we are eternally grateful! In Your Name, Amen!

CALL TO ACTION

Take some time to think about your friends, family members, neighbors, coworkers who do not know the Lord. Make a list, and commit to praying for them on a regular basis. Pray for opportunities to share the gospel with them.

READY, SET, GO!

CHAPTER 14

JESUS, THE LIVING WATER

"But whoever drinks of the water that I shall give him will never thirst. But the water that I shall give him will become in him a fountain of water springing up into everlasting life." (John 4:14)

AH, THERE IS NOTHING LIKE a tall glass of iced tea on a hot summer day. When the heat is parching your throat, that icy cold beverage soothes and satisfies you. Warm drinks simply don't cut it. But no matter how satisfying it is while you are drinking it, sooner or later you are going to need to replenish your glass and quench the thirst again.

Jesus speaks of a different kind of thirst-the longing of the soul that the world can't satisfy. In John 4:5-30, we read the story of the "woman at the well". Essentially Jesus teaches the Samaritan woman that the water she is searching for is not physical, but spiritual. As we read the exchange, we come to understand that she has been living a life devoid of happiness and joy. She has been searching for earthly satisfaction when what she needed was Jesus.

What exactly does the Bible mean when it speaks of living water? It is the power of the Holy Spirit working in and flowing out of the life of a believer. When we decide to follow Jesus, the Holy Spirit comes and dwells within us. So how does that look practically? Well, first we need to understand the function of the Holy Spirit.

The Holy Spirit is not just some spiritual being that floats around. He is the third member of the Holy Trinity-God the Father, God the Son, and God the Spirit. After Jesus rose from the dead, He ascended to heaven. In

His place came the Holy Spirit. And through that Spirit, the apostles who had spent three years under the teaching of Jesus (wouldn't that have been amazing!) were equipped with mighty gifts and abilities. They gained a boldness to preach the gospel that they never had before. He was the helper Jesus referred to at the beginning of Acts.

The Holy Spirit gives gifts to us today as well. Teaching, hospitality, wisdom, and discernment, to name a few. When we receive Jesus as our Lord and Savior, the Spirit indwells us and lives in our hearts. He also has the power to convict us of sin and to help us to understand scripture. He gives us words to say in given situations. He corrects us, encourages us, and guides us in all truth. So, as you can see, He is a powerful member of the heavenly Trinity. Jesus referred to the Holy Spirit as the Living Water.

Can we have this same power that the apostles had? Some scholars have argued that the Apostolic age, when the apostles were sharing and preaching, was a very specific time when the gifts and power of the Spirit were given, and do not apply today. Well, I am in the camp that believes that the gifts of the Spirit are alive and active today. The Holy Spirit has been carrying on the ministry of Jesus in and through believers since 33 A.D. If you were to remove the Spirit, then what would be dwelling in our hearts? Our flesh would be running amok. It is the living water of the Holy Spirit that is renewing us day by day and working in our hearts to keep us on that narrow path. The Bible speaks of the Living Water many times. Here are several passages to consider:

"He who believes in Me, as the Scripture has said, out of his heart will flow rivers of living water." (John 7:38) When we become followers of Jesus, the spiritual blessings that we receive will flow out of us and onto others. The power of the Holy Spirit will be working in and through us.

"The Lord is my shepherd; I shall not want. He makes me to lie down in green pastures; He leads me beside the still waters." (Psalm 23:1-2) We have everything we need in Him. He gives us comfort, rest, and peace.

"As the deer pants for the water brooks, so pants my soul for You, O God. My soul thirsts for God, for the living God. When shall I come

and appear before God?" (Psalm 42:1-2) We have a longing for fellowship with God. And only He can satisfy those deep needs of the soul.

"O God, You are my God; early will I seek You; my soul thirsts for You; my flesh longs for You in a dry and thirsty land where there is no water." (Psalm 63:1) There are times when life feels so barren and dry. But we can come to the fountain and drink deeply and fully, and receive total restoration.

"Therefore with joy, you will draw water from the wells of salvation." (Isaiah 12:3) What an awesome thing that we can freely come to the well and drink of the Living Water. We don't have to buy it, order it, or even stand in line for it. We simply cry out to the Living God.

"On the last day, that great day of the feast, Jesus stood and cried out, saying, 'If anyone thirsts, let him come to Me and drink.'" (John 7:37) At the last day of the feast, Jesus was calling them to Him. They did not understand that He was speaking of the Holy Spirit and not of physical water.

"Let us draw near with a true heart in full assurance of faith, having our hearts sprinkled from an evil conscience and our bodies washed with pure water." (Hebrews 10:22) Nothing feels better than to take a shower after you have become dirty or sweaty. It is so refreshing and renewing. When we draw near to Jesus, He washes and cleanses our hearts and minds. Through Him, we can be squeaky clean on the inside!

"Then I will sprinkle clean water on you, and you shall be clean; I will cleanse you from all your filthiness and from all your idols." (Ezekiel 36:25) In this passage, God was speaking of Israel's spiritual regeneration. It applies to us as well. We need to be rid of the filth of sin and idols.

"For the Lamb who is in the midst of the throne will shepherd them and lead them to living fountains of waters. And God will wipe away every tear from their eyes." (Revelation 7:17) This passage speaks of the

believers who will come out of the Great Tribulation. They have endured much hardship, but God will reward them, replenish them, and there will be no more tears.

"And He said to me, 'It is done! I am the Alpha and the Omega, the Beginning and the End. I will give of the fountain of the water of life freely to him who thirsts.'" (Revelation 21:6) At this point, after the Tribulation period and Christ's 1,000-year reign, Jesus is declaring that all that He set out to accomplish was completed. And all who have been saved by His grace will never thirst again.

"And Jesus said to them, 'I am the bread of life. He who comes to Me shall never hunger, and he who believes in Me shall never thirst.'" (John 6:35) Jesus is saying that whoever comes to Him will have their spiritual hunger filled and their thirst forever quenched. We are so preoccupied at times with our physical needs and discomfort when those needs are not met. But what we need to be concerned with is our spiritual needs. The physical is temporary. But the spiritual has eternal implications.

"Ho! Everyone who thirsts, come to the waters; and you who have no money, come, buy and eat. Yes, come, buy wine and milk without money and without price." (Isaiah 55:1) We used to sing this scripture at a church I went to years ago. I never gave much thought to what we were singing. But here, God is telling Israel to return to Him. The gift He was offering was free. If we were offered that by some street vendor, we would be wondering what the catch was!

But there's no catch with Jesus. Because the price was already paid. God is calling us to freely come to the fountain of eternal life with Him. He gives us all the food and water that we will ever need spiritually. It is the most important thing we can ever have. Everything else is just stuff that gets in the way of that free-flowing fountain of love.

"And the Spirit and the bride say, 'Come!' And let him who hears say, 'Come!' And let him who thirsts come. Whoever desires, let him take the water of life freely." (Revelation 22:17)

BIBLE STUDY AND JOURNAL TIME

Grab your bible, and dig into the chapter's scriptures! Don't forget to read the entire chapter to get the context. And record what the Lord has revealed to you in each passage. Pray for revelation before you begin.

JOHN 4:14 ("Anchor" passage)

_____
_____
_____
_____
_____
_____
_____
_____

JOHN 7:38

_____
_____
_____
_____
_____
_____
_____
_____

PSALM 23:1-2

_____
_____
_____
_____
_____
_____
_____
_____

PSALM 42:1-2

_____
_____
_____
_____
_____
_____
_____
_____

PSALM 63:1

_____
_____
_____
_____
_____
_____
_____

ISAIAH 12:3

_____
_____
_____
_____
_____
_____
_____
_____

JOHN 7:37

_____
_____
_____
_____
_____
_____
_____
_____
_____

HEBREWS 10:22

_____
_____
_____
_____
_____
_____
_____
_____
_____

EZEKIEL 36:25

_____
_____
_____
_____
_____
_____
_____
_____
_____

REVELATION 7:17

_____

_____

_____

_____

_____

_____

_____

_____

REVELATION 21:6

_____

_____

_____

_____

_____

_____

_____

JOHN 6:35

_____

_____

_____

_____

_____

_____

_____

ISAIAH 55:1

_____
_____
_____
_____
_____
_____
_____
_____

REVELATION 22:17

_____
_____
_____
_____
_____
_____
_____
_____

Now, summarize below what you have learned through the passages. Look for a common theme.

_____

_____

_____

_____

_____

_____

_____

_____

_____

_____

_____

_____

_____

_____

_____

_____

_____

_____

_____

_____

_____

_____

_____

_____

_____

_____

_____

_____

_____

REFLECTION TIME

Has there been a time when you were spiritually dry?

_____

_____

_____

_____

_____

How does reading the Word resolve that dryness?

_____

_____

_____

_____

_____

How do the scriptures in this chapter minister to you?

_____

_____

_____

_____

_____

Write out a prayer thanking God for His free, flowing cleansing water.

_____

_____

_____

_____

_____

_____

Dear Heavenly Father:

Thank you so much that You can bring refreshing water when we are in a dry parched wilderness. Help us to always seek You when we are in need of a time of refreshing and hydration of Your Word. In Your name, Amen!

CALL TO ACTION

Do a deep dive into the story of the woman at the well. Can you relate to her? Was there a time before you became a Christian where you were searching for the world to satisfy your needs? How do you see it differently now? Journal your thoughts.

READY, SET, GO!

CHAPTER 15

GIRD UP YOUR LOINS

"Therefore gird up the loins of your mind, be sober, and rest your hope fully upon the grace that is to be brought to you at the revelation of Jesus Christ" (1 Peter 1:13)

NOW THAT WE ARE FULLY equipped with God's Word, it is time to move forward as a member of the army of the Lord! When we became Christians, we were drafted into that army. Satan has put a big bullseye on our backs. He will constantly be shooting fiery darts at us. But with God's Word in our hearts, we are fully armed to deflect them.

What does it mean to gird up the loins? In Old Testament days, men wore long robes. If they needed to move more freely or engage in battle, they would take the bottom of the robe, pull it up between their legs and tuck it into their belts, thus allowing for more freedom of movement.

To gird up the loins of our mind is to be prepared for action while being alert and sober in our spirit. We are living in precarious times, where God's Word has been distorted and twisted to adapt to every deviant behavior. We are warned to take heed that we don't get caught up in the doctrine of false teachers. The only way we can do that is to know God's Word. We need to be in it daily. Not to just read it academically, but to study it. An interesting bit of information for you-when bank tellers are trained to find counterfeit money, the first thing they are taught is to be so familiar with the real ones that they can instantly spot the fake. So it should be with us. Please, do not spend a lot of time studying the false teachings of cults without a strong knowledge of the truth of God's Word. Satan is a master at deception. You can read the cult's "beliefs" and they appear to line up with ours. If you don't know the Word well, you'll get sucked into the lie.

"Blessed is the man who walks not in the counsel of the ungodly, nor stands in the path of sinners, nor sits in the seat of the scornful; but his delight is in the law of the Lord, and in His law he meditates day and night. He shall be like a tree planted by the rivers of water, that brings forth its fruit in its season, whose leaf also shall not wither; and whatever he does shall prosper." (Psalm 1:1-3) That's the key. Be in the Word daily, meditate on what it says, pray for the Holy Spirit to give you clarity, and then apply what you learned to your life. You will then be able to bear much fruit.

"Your Word is a lamp to my feet and a light to my path." (Psalm 119:105) The inerrant Word of God will always show us how to walk in His light. We will be able to walk that narrow path. Because the road IS narrow. But our footing is sure when we are grounded in the Bible.

It's also important that we study the entire counsel of God. Some churches do not teach the Old Testament, arguing that we are not under the old covenant of the law, but under the new covenant of grace. But the OT lays the foundation for the NT. Jesus, Himself, quoted from the OT 78 times. And yes, you will find Jesus throughout the 39 NT books. It has been said that the OT is Christ concealed, and the NT is Christ revealed. The Bible is the story of Jesus, from Genesis 1 to Revelation 22. Don't cheat yourself by skipping books.

"The grass withers, the flower fades, but the Word of our God stands forever." (Isaiah 40:8) The beautiful thing about the Bible is that everything else comes and goes, but God's Word is the same yesterday, today, and forever.

"For the word of God is living and powerful, and sharper than any two-edged sword, piercing even to the division of soul and spirit, and of joints and marrow, and is a discerner of the thoughts and intents of the heart." (Hebrews 4:12) Ooh, ouch on that last part! We don't like having our sins exposed, even to ourselves. But you will never grow in your walk with Jesus, and live a life pleasing to Him unless you cut out the

dead parts of your heart. And sin destroys. Remember, God's Word is the Living Water that cleanses and purifies us.

"Sanctify them by Your truth. Your Word is truth." (John 17:17) To sanctify is to set apart. We have been set apart from the world to be equipped and be usable vessels for God's work. Notice it doesn't say the word has truth. It says it IS truth.

"*But sanctify the Lord God in your hearts, and always be ready to give a defense to everyone who asks you a reason for the hope that is in you, with meekness and fear."* (1 Peter 3:15) And now that we have allowed God into our hearts and we are studying the Word, we can confidently share with others why we have this blessed hope when the world around us is in chaos.

"Be diligent to present yourself approved to God, a worker who does not need to be ashamed, rightly dividing the word of truth." (2 Timothy 2:15) Never be ashamed of who you are in Christ. We have the answer to life everlasting. And if we are speaking the truth of God's Word, we will always have His approval. But remember to always speak the truth with love.

"All Scripture is given by inspiration of God, and is profitable for doctrine, for reproof, for correction, for instruction in righteousness, that the man of God may be complete, thoroughly equipped for every good work." (2 Timothy 3:16-17) Did you know that all scripture was breathed by God? Not just some of it. ALL of it. And we need to learn the entire counsel of God. It is our instruction manual for life. Do not think that you can't find truth on every page. Because it is there. Admittedly, some of it may seem repetitious and tedious to read. But the nuggets are there, I promise you!

"Your Word I have hidden in my heart, That I might not sin against You." (Psalm 119:11) The only way we can lead a life that is pleasing to God is to learn and apply His Word daily.

I would be remiss if I didn't address the subject of spiritual warfare. Because, like I said earlier, we are hip deep in the battle for our fellow man.

"For we do not wrestle against flesh and blood, but against principalities, against powers, against the rulers of the darkness of this age, against spiritual hosts of wickedness in the heavenly places. Therefore take up the whole armor of God, that you may be able to withstand in the evil day, and having done all, to stand." (Ephesians 6:12-13) First of all, it is vital to recognize who our adversary is. It is not our fellow man. Our true enemy is Satan and all his cohorts. They are an evil and destructive bunch. And those who are not believers are his puppets. Satan will use any method he can to disrupt, destroy, and discredit us. He hates anything that God loves.

"Stand therefore, having girded your waist with truth, having put on the breastplate of righteousness, and having shod your feet with the preparation of the gospel of peace; above all, taking the shield of faith with which you will be able to quench all the fiery darts of the wicked one. And take the helmet of salvation, and the sword of the Spirit, which is the Word of God; praying always with all prayer and supplication in the Spirit, being watchful to this end with all perseverance and supplication for all the saints." (Ephesians 6:14-18) The second part of the passage shows us how to equip ourselves for the battle. Take some extra time and do a study on each piece of our arsenal.

"For the time will come when they will not endure sound doctrine, but according to their own desires, because they have itching ears, they will heap up for themselves teachers; and they will turn their ears away from the truth, and be turned aside to fables. But you be watchful in all things, endure afflictions, do the work of an evangelist, fulfill your ministry." (2 Timothy 4:3-5) The time is here, folks! People only want to hear what makes them feel good about themselves, about how God can make their life better. They don't want to talk about sin. They would rather stay in their comfortable lives. But we have the key to a fulfilling and fruitful life. It is the power of God's Word. Let's not hide our lamp under a basket, okay?

"Fight the good fight of faith, lay hold on eternal life, to which you were also called and have confessed the good confession in the presence of many witnesses." (1 Timothy 6:12)

BIBLE STUDY AND JOURNAL TIME

Grab your bible, and dig into the chapter's scriptures! Don't forget to read the entire chapter to get the context. And record what the Lord has revealed to you in each passage. Pray for revelation before you begin.

1 PETER 1:13 ("Anchor" passage)

_____
_____
_____
_____
_____
_____
_____
_____

PSALM 1:1-3

_____
_____
_____
_____
_____
_____
_____
_____

PSALM 119:105

_____
_____
_____
_____
_____
_____
_____

ISAIAH 40:8

_____

_____

_____

_____

_____

_____

_____

_____

_____

HEBREWS 4:12

_____

_____

_____

_____

_____

_____

_____

_____

JOHN 17:17

_____

_____

_____

_____

_____

_____

_____

_____

_____

1 PETER 3:15

_____
_____
_____
_____
_____
_____
_____
_____

2 TIMOTHY 2:15

_____
_____
_____
_____
_____
_____
_____
_____

2 TIMOTHY 3:16-17

_____
_____
_____
_____
_____
_____
_____
_____

PSALM 119:11

_____

_____

_____

_____

_____

_____

_____

_____

_____

EPHESIANS 6:12-13

_____

_____

_____

_____

_____

_____

_____

_____

EPHESIANS 6:14-18

_____

_____

_____

_____

_____

_____

_____

_____

_____

2 TIMOTHY 4:3-5

_____
_____
_____
_____
_____
_____
_____
_____
_____
_____

1 TIMOTHY 6:12

_____
_____
_____
_____
_____
_____
_____
_____
_____
_____

Now, summarize below what you have learned through the passages. Look for a common theme.

_____

_____

_____

_____

_____

_____

_____

_____

_____

_____

_____

_____

_____

_____

_____

_____

_____

_____

_____

_____

_____

_____

_____

_____

_____

_____

_____

_____

_____

_____

REFLECTION TIME

Have you been able to meet the challenge of studying all the passages?

_____

_____

_____

_____

_____

_____

How do you view God's Word in light of your new knowledge?

_____

_____

_____

_____

_____

_____

How are you more equipped to share God's Word?

_____

_____

_____

_____

_____

_____

Write out a prayer thanking God for His Word for us.

_____

_____

_____

_____

_____

_____

_____

Dear Heavenly Father:

Thank You that Your Word is true. Thank You that it never changes. It is a true constant in this ever-changing world we live in. But we know that what You say will always apply to our lives. Help us to be diligent in studying it and seeking You every single day. In Your name, Amen!

CALL TO ACTION

Review the passages throughout our study. What chapter spoke to your heart the most? Are there areas that you may not have studied as much as the others? Make a study plan to reinforce what you have learned and to increase your knowledge in areas that you are weak.

READY, SET, GO!

CONCLUSION

WELL, WE MADE IT! FIFTEEN chapters and 210 different bible passages. I pray that this journey has been fruitful for you.

I encourage you to continue seeking God through His Word. No matter how much time you spend reading and studying it, there will always be new golden nuggets to uncover.

My last challenge for you is to create a study plan for your daily time in God's Word. This can take on a variety of formats. Here are some suggestions

- Choose a book of the Bible, read through it and outline it, chapter by chapter
- Do topical studies. For example, dig into the Armor of God or the Beatitudes from the Sermon on the Mount
- Learn about all the attributes of God.
- Study the various prayers
- Choose topics like we studied and create your own scripture passage list.

The choices are endless. The important thing is to meet God on a regular basis in His Word. But always pray first before you begin your adventure.

Speaking of adventures, I am working on my next one. I am elbow deep into the next book, a family friendly devotional series through the Bible, starting at the best place, Genesis 1! We will explore all the popular bible stories, and hit on some jewels that may not be so familiar. I hope you come along for the ride. Actually, I have more than one in progress, so you will just have to stay tuned!

One parting scripture, on the house! As you continue to draw closer to the Lord, this is my prayer for you:

"Therefore, as the elect of God, holy and beloved, put on tender mercies, kindness, humility, meekness, longsuffering; bearing with one another, and forgiving one another, if anyone has a complaint against another; even as Christ forgave you, so you also must do. But above all these things put on love, which is the bond of perfection. And let the peace of God rule in your hearts, to which also you were called in one body; and be thankful. Let the Word of Christ dwell in you richly in all wisdom, teaching and admonishing one another in psalms and hymns and spiritual songs, singing with grace in your hearts to the Lord. And whatever you do in word or deed, do all in the name of the Lord Jesus, giving thanks to God the Father through Him." (Colossians 3:12-17)

God bless you!

Deborah Bedson

ADDITIONAL TITLES BY DEBORAH BEDSON

Please check out my devotional Series

"It's All About Jesus the Living Word" Volumes 1 and 2.

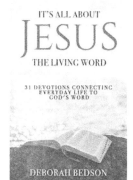

Volume 1 contains 31 easy-to-read devotionals with anecdotal stories that will help you to apply God's Word to everyday life.

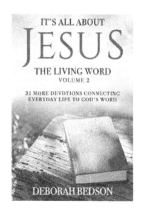

Volume 2 picks up where Volume 1 left off, with 31 more stories and scriptures to explore. Each book has bible verses written out, reflection questions and a call to action.

Both books are available from the following websites:

- Amazon.com
- Barnesandnoble.com

JOIN THE JOURNEY

The Christian walk is not an easy one, and we were not meant to go it alone. As the Bible says, iron sharpens iron, and a three-cord strand is not easily broken. I invite you to join me as we travel along on this journey.

Please check out my social media sites:

www.deborahbedsonauthor.com   Here you will get updates on my new projects, find recommended resources and a sign up for my weekly emails. There is also a weekly memory verse page.

www.letstalkaboutjesusblog.blogspot.com catch up on my weekly blog posts about life with Jesus, weekly bible memory verses and other cool stuff!

Join my Facebook group, **It's All About Jesus The Living Word.** Here we share updates, prayer requests and praise reports, and have a fun time interacting with other believers, encouraging and strengthening the brethren! But mostly it is a place where Jesus is honored.

I look forward to meeting you there!

If you have any questions or comments please email me at:

deborah@deborahbedsonauthor.com

ABOUT THE AUTHOR

Deborah Bedson is a native of Southern California and grew up in a home that loved Jesus. Desiring to get out of the rat race of the big city and longing for a more rural lifestyle, she moved to the northern farmlands of Washington State in 2015. There she fell in love with the beauty of God's creation. Time spent working in the Christian retail industry increased her love for spreading the Word of God. After many encouraging words from family and friends to write (and much prayer about how to do this!) Deborah launched her new writing career with "It's All About Jesus the Living Word". It is her prayer that through her writings, the reader will develop a deeper, more meaningful connection with God.

Made in the USA
Middletown, DE
05 November 2023

41865842R00109